I hope you enjoy
this book.

Charlotte Schmidt
2018

love is a family:

Memoir of a Lifetime

By
Charlotte Adele Schwab
Schmidt

SAOIRSE PRESS
Vancouver   Dublin   London

Cover: Picture: From page 156 of this book: Charlotte, Ric, and Lois's daughter Gayle.
Cover design by Adam Webber. Thank you, Adam, for your awesome design, for your
wisdom, and for all your hard work! And thanks for letting me hold Aurora whenever I
want!
Copy editing by: Adele Smith. Thank you for such a quick turn-around, working hard
even during Rosa and TJs reception. You're the best copy editor/nurse I know!
Flourishes purchased from Adobe

Amy Webber
Saoirse Press
6101 NE 38th Place
Vancouver, WA 98661

This book is dedicated to Norm.

Table of Contents

Introduction

Welcome to my mother's memoir, a place centered in love and where every story intertwines. Enjoy reading about events young Charlotte witnesses and lives as they influence her later stories in unexpected ways. Through this grand memoir that covers from before she was born until present day, we are reminded to cherish these types of connections and see them in our own lives.

Mom's direct and compassionate voice creates a world, a glimpse of the past, that would otherwise be lost if she hadn't shared her stories. She invites you into her life; to laugh and cry and become invested in the lives of those she has loved. She presents their truth as one of faith and inspiration.

Charlotte Adele Schwab Schmidt is the most extraordinary woman I know, and it's not just because she's my mother. Watching her interact with people through the years has shown me what grace and love is all about. Her stories are equally enchanting as she brings her positive elegance onto each page.

It's been my pleasure to compile, edit, and design this book. As a reader, you are now a part of the story and a member of our family. For us, family is what it's all about and Charlotte is the life and love of our family.

Amy Schmidt Webber

Paul and Eleanor

The Mayor's Handsome Son and the Silver Miner's Beautiful Daughter

The Mayor's Son

Paul Francis Schwab was born June 24, 1902 in Mt. Angel, Oregon. He was the sixth child of Fred and Anna Mary (Mayer) Schwab. He had four sisters and one brother older than him, and two sisters and two brothers younger than him.

Paul at 14 ½ in 1916

Paul attended grade school first through eighth grade in Mt. Angel. He then worked with his father in the family business. His father, Fred, had been the first mayor of Mt. Angel and had established the Fred Schwab Commission Company, a feed and seed warehouse. Years later, when he became the manager, Paul visited the local farmers during the hop season to determine when the crops would be ready for harvest and how much space in the warehouse would be needed for the baled hops to be stored.

Paul

Paul was the son in the family who could meet anyone with a smile and a friendly handshake. He truly enjoyed meeting anyone who had just moved to town, welcoming them and learning all about them and their families. As the town was so small, he walked around and greeted everyone with an affectionate teasing manner.

Paul loved children and when he walked home for lunch he would stop at his older sister's houses to see the children of the families.

One day, two of Fred's granddaughters were playing inside the cool warehouse building and saw some grapes in one of the back rooms. She put a finger into the juice that was being squeezed from the grapes and it tasted like vinegar. The girls concluded that Grandpa also sold vinegar.

The oldest son Joe had moved to California and opened a potato cleaning and bagging business. The other three sons were active in their father's Mt. Angel warehouse operation. They spent long hours in the warehouse during the growing season.

The young men of the town were volunteer fire fighters. If they needed more help with the field fires or a barn fire, the departments from Monitor, Marquam or the larger units from Silverton or Woodburn would send assistance.

John Bigler, Jody Miller, Leo Schwab, Albin Butsch, Joe Wachter, Caspar Terhaar, Paul Schwab, Laurence Travis, Joe Berchtold, Joe Ficker. Sitting: All Ficker, Emil Schurbach

Besides fighting fires, cleaning the fire trucks after each use, and other community celebrations with the local flax festival and church activities, the young men of the town were business owners and farmers.

As most of them were descendants of the German families who settled this area of Marion County, they often celebrated by having family parties and dances. They had plenty of food and the preferred drink was beer.

Most Saturday nights the dance hall at Broadacres, a few miles away, was filled with local young people from Mt. Angel, Woodburn, Silverton, Monitor, Marquam, St Paul and other small towns along highway 99.

Paul and his brothers Leo and Louis joined the others, sometimes with a date and sometimes single, as the girls would also be there without dates.

The Silver Miner's Daughter

Eleanor's father, Frank W. Fischer, was born in 1876 in Racine, Wisconsin. He was the third child of Jacob Franz and Christina Fischer. His father died when Frank was just eleven years old. Left a widow, his mother "gathered up her little flock in 1893, and removed to Oregon," settling on a farm outside Mt. Angel. He married Veronica (also known as Verona) Hassing in 1900. By 1910, they had three children and were living in Portland, Oregon. Their first child, Edward, died in April 1911 from septic poisoning and acute osteomyelitis. He was 7 years old. In Nov. 1911, they had a fourth child, Raymond.

In 1920, they lived in Ketchikan, Alaska with Eleanor 13, Leonard 10, and Raymond 8. What an exciting venture this must have been!

Frank was the tram superintendent at the Premier Mine Company in Hyder, Alaska for 30 years before they moved to Mt. Angel, Oregon to be close to their children

Top pictures: Premier Mine Company.

who had moved there. While in Hyder, they had two foster children, Tom Jabrow and Jewel Rice. Since it was so difficult for the children to get to school on a daily basis, they lived in the larger town of Ketchikan, Alaska during the school year and moved back to Hyder during the summer.

Today, Hyder, Alaska is almost as small as it was when my grandparents lived there. According to Wikipedia, their 2010 census said they had 87 residents. The ferry they rode to Ketchikan for school stopped running in the 1990s. Hyder is Alaska's most southernmost and easternmost town that's 75 miles away from Ketchikan by air and 405 miles by car.

Postcard: Tongass Tribe Totem Pole in Hyder, Alaska.

After Eleanor graduated from high school on May 15, 1924 in Ketchikan, she continued her education in Mt. Angel, Oregon attending Mt. Angel Normal School where she graduated on June 15, 1926 with credentials to become an elementary school teacher.

Eleanor and her doll.

Eleanor's two younger brothers attended Washington State College in Pullman, Washington. Leonard became a pharmacist, owning his pharmacy in downtown Mt. Angel, Oregon. Raymond joined the U.S. Corps of Engineers after graduation.

He and his family were stationed in Army bases all over the world.

Eleanor chose the Mt. Angel Normal School and its location because her Mother's sister, Rose, was a student at the college and lived in a home nearby.

Mt. Angel Normal School

After Eleanor graduated, she was accepted to teach a year at the grade school in Powers, a small town in southwestern Oregon. The valley is encircled by mountains and the train system was its only method of transportation.

Eleanor shared a house with the other single ladies who were also hired to teach that year in Powers. Since she didn't have any sisters, living with seven other girls was fun for her. She communicated with each of them by mail frequently throughout the years afterwards.

After they had been in their new teaching positions for

Eleanor in Powers

a couple of months, the ladies decided to invite the young men (who they had been dating) to dinner at their house. The ladies all had ideas of what to fix to make a memorable meal for their guests.

Eleanor's friends

Apparently, some of these teachers were also jokesters and they decided to play a trick on the men. They acquired some small blocks of wood the size of the French cakes called "petit fours." They then frosted the wood all around, put small flowers on the top of each, and let the frosting dry. When dessert time came, the ladies brought each guest a colorfully decorated "cake".

The ladies sneaked outside and looked through the windows to watch for the reaction of their guests. The laughter that followed the trick shook the entire house.

Eleanor

The summer after she taught school in Powers, Eleanor took the train to Vancouver, B.C. and boarded the ship to Alaska to visit her parents. When she arrived, her parents greeted her warmly but when her Mother saw that she had cut her hair in the "bobbed" style of the 20's, reports are that her Mother became very angry. She had liked the long hair that her only daughter had worn since she was a child.

After a visit with her family, Eleanor took the ship back to Vancouver, B.C. and the train back to Oregon.

As the college that Eleanor attended was in the same town where Paul lived, it was inevitable that they would meet.

Eleanor and Paul

As they dated, they went to the dances with all the other young couples from the valley and dated for many months.

Eleanor and Paul's wedding November 14, 1928

Then, on Wednesday, November 14, 1928 at 8:15am, during a wedding mass at St. Mary's Church in Mt. Angel, Oregon, Marion County, Paul Francis Schwab, 26 years old, and Eleanor Barbara Fisher, 23 years old, were married.

Paul and Eleanor's Honeymoon

Along with their wedding and honeymoon plans, Paul and Eleanor needed to find a place to live while their home in Mt. Angel was being built. They chose to rent a furnished house on the corner close to the warehouse, where he worked.

Eleanor

As a wedding present, Grandpa Schwab gave each of his children a plot of land not far from their parent's home. Paul's lot was three blocks from his parents. (Rose and Leo each had their lots across from Paul. Louis' lot was next to his cousin Herman's. Mary's home was three blocks south of the warehouse. Joe and his sister Bertha were in

Stockton, California. Agnes and her family also lived in California. The youngest daughter, Amanda, chose the property one block from her parent's home and Gertrude's home was across the road from her parent's home.)

Another wedding present was from Paul's business friend from Silverton. He gave the young couple a gift of a night at their beach home in Neskowin, Oregon.

After the wedding and all the celebrations, Paul and Eleanor left for their honeymoon. Their car had various cans and other noisy metals attached to the back bumper so as they drove away, the noise followed their car down the road. This was a custom at this time and it made everyone laugh.

Eleanor's friends with Eleanor and Paul

The next day, their journey continued south. Highway 101 along the Coast Highway did not have bridges until 1935. So, as each section of the highway ended at a river that flowed through the state on the way to the Pacific Ocean, cars crossed the rivers on a ferry.

Their next destination was Powers, where Eleanor had taught school for a year. She wanted to introduce her new husband to all her friends that she had met there. After a few pictures were taken and a tour through the small town, they continued their journey to see Paul's brother and sisters and their families in California.

They visited the mission at Santa Barbara and took pictures of all the places they visited.

They were gone three weeks before they returned to Mt. Angel.

Eleanor in Santa Barbara

Paul and Eleanor in Santa Barbara vineyards

No. *16990*

Marriage Certificate

State of Oregon, } ss.
County of Marion, }

THIS IS TO CERTIFY that the undersigned,

a *Catholic priest*

by authority of a license bearing date the

16th day of *Nov.* 192*5*

and issued by the County Clerk of the County of

Marion, did, on the *14th*

day of *Nov.* 192*5* at the

in the County and State aforesaid, join in lawful

wedlock *Paul F. Schwab*
NAME OF MALE

_____ of the County of Marion

_____ and State of Oregon

_____ and

Eleanor Fisher
NAME OF FEMALE

of the County of ~~Marion,~~

and the ~~State of Oregon~~ *Alaska Territory*
with their mutual assent, in the presence of

Rose A. Schwab
Leonard N. Fisher
Witnesses

My Certificate of Authority to solemnize mar-

riage is recorded in *Marion*
County, Oregon.
Witness my hand

ST. MARY'S PARISH.

F. Demme O.S.B. PASTOR

This Certificate to be filled out by officer or clergyman and given to
the parties who have been married.

Paul and Eleanor's marriage certificate

part

one

The Early

Years

September Morn

I was born on Friday, September 6, 1929 in the Silverton Hospital a few miles away from my home in Mt. Angel, Oregon. I weighed 8 pounds 12 ounces. For the records, I always say that I was born in Mt. Angel instead of Silverton because that's where the family lived. Nobody really cares. By this

Paul and Eleanor with Charlotte in 1929

time in my life I have had to identify myself so many times and no one has ever noticed the difference. I had black hair, kind of curly (there is a snip of my first haircut in my baby book), and brown eyes. My father had black naturally curly hair and I have always wanted to have naturally curly hair.

Eleanor in a hat and Paul with his naturally curly hair.

I found a poem in my baby book that was written by Paul's brother Joe on the occasion of my birth. I don't remember Joe very well, I just remember that he and his family lived way far away, and we seldom saw them.

Charlotte Adele; oh what bliss!
Eight 3/4 pound of pure loveliness
Slumbering in a snowy Eiderdown bundle,
For Mama & Papa to joy o'er and trundle.

As I gaze upon the picture where she sleeps,
Apprehension and Wonderment over one creeps:
Had you forgotten? You surely skipped
To mention:— "She is with a Selfstarter equipped"

If not; buy her a Japanese Musical "Rattle"
So she'll wake; and we enjoy her sweet baby prattle
By the time I come to Mt. Angel, to tease her,
Make her laugh and hug and squeeze her.

In the Meantime, tell her:
"Hello"
From her loving Uncle
Joe.

Charlotte Adele; oh what bliss!
Eight ¾ pound of pure loveliness
Slumbering in a snowy Eiderdown bundle,
For Mama & Papa to joy ov'r and trundle.

As I gaze from the picture where she sleeps,
Apprehension and Wonderment over me creeps:
Had you forgotten? You surely skipped
To mention: - "She is with a selfstarter" equipped.

If not; buy her a Japanese (?) Musical Rattle
So she'll wake; and we enjoy her sweet baby prattle
By the time I come to Mt. Angel, to tease her,
Make her laugh and hug and squeeze her.

In the meantime, tell her:
"Hello"
From her loving Uncle
Joe.

According to my baby book, both my Mother and Father named me, and I think that Mother suggested the name Charlotte because of the Queen Charlotte Islands. She had taken the passenger ship to visit her parents so frequently from Vancouver, B.C. to Hyder, Alaska that she had sailed by the Queen Charlotte Islands many, many times. My middle name is Adele and I know that was the name of

Paul on the left, Paul's mother Anna Mary (Mayer) Schwab holding Charlotte, and Eleanor is on the right

a friend of Aunt Bertha's whom they met on their honeymoon while visiting in California.

Charlotte is a big name for a little girl, but I began to like it because no one else had that unusual of a name. I wouldn't meet another Charlotte in school until I was a senior in high school. (In later years, when we lived in Louisiana, I would hear someone call out my name and invariably it was a Mother calling her small daughter.)

Eleanor and Charlotte with Mary Schwab LeDoux and Richard

I was baptized on September 8, 1929 at St. Mary's Church, Mt. Angel, Oregon by Father Dominic, Pastor. My father recorded ten lines of friends and relatives who attended.

Charlotte

Eleanor and Charlotte

Pictures of Charlotte.

Bottom right: Charlotte and Lois sitting on house banisters. Charlotte on the right and Lois on the left.

My sister Lois Eleanor was born on April 16, 1931. My sister Marlene Irma was born on November 16, 1934. My brother Ronald Edward was born on April 12, 1939.

Herbert Hoover was inaugurated as President in March 1929. In October, the United States Stock Market crashed on

Charlotte and Lois, 1931

"Black Tuesday". It must have made an impact on our small community. Dad always planted a garden and we raised potatoes, carrots, peas, corn, beans, tomatoes, etc. This helped our family and community during the depression.

On the back of our property was a chicken coop. The chickens inside supplied our eggs and, at a certain time of the month, our meat. A chicken was killed, and the feathers removed in preparation for a good meal. We would also put the meat in a rented freezer at the creamery along with beef or pork which was purchased from friends or relatives on the farm.

All the families in the town and surrounding areas had the

September 1935

same since the homes always had a large enough area for a garden and chicken coop.

In a certain grade in school we learned about the bartering system. We understood that it was a system that worked very well when money was not available.

Black Tuesday hit Wall Street on October 29, 1929. Billions of dollars were lost that day as investors traded about 16 million shares on the New York Stock Exchange. America and the rest of the industrialized world dove into the Great Depression because of this. It lasted from1929-1939 and was the longest-lasting economic downturn in the history of the Western industrialized world. Charlotte's family wasn't the only family who used the barter system and other creative ways to get the goods and services they needed. It was a time when people all over the country had to help each other and find creative ways to support their families. *

Home

On November 15, 1931, our parents started an account for their new home. First, they hired an architect for $25.00 and ordered $72.60 worth of gravel delivered to their property, which was located about 4 blocks down from the church. The

Paul, Lois, Charlotte, and Eleanor in front of their new home.

building project was completed in time for our family to move in June 1932. At this time, I was almost 3 years old, and Lois would be 2 on her next birthday. Our family had been living in a rental home across from Grandpa's warehouse. Our new home had a basement with a furnace and a wood stove. There was a room for the washing machine and stationary tubs. The room had a high ceiling with laundry lines to hang the wash on rainy days. Also, there was plenty of room for the children to play inside on a rainy day.

When the weather turned very warm, we brought our bedding down to the basement. That was always fun times for little girls. We could pretend it was a fairyland or other places our imagination took us. Then Mother or Daddy would call from upstairs, "Girls, it's time for you go to sleep!!!!"

Eleanor with Charlotte, Lois, Dolly, and Teddy Bear in front of new home in Mt. Angel.

The main floor included a bedroom, a bathroom, a small playroom, a kitchen with a wood stove, and a breakfast nook that had a swinging door into the dining room and living room.

Up the stairs from the living room were two more large bedrooms, a bathroom, and a small open room at the top of the stairs.

Article in the Mt. Angel News about Miss Charlotte Schwab's 4th birthday party.

The house was very well designed. It was large and roomy and a safe and comfortable place in which to grow up. We moved in when I was almost three years old and we moved out when I was almost fifteen years old. The house has survived very well and seems to still be well taken care of.

The plan to put a wood stove in the basement was an inspired idea. Every family canned fruits, vegetables, and even meats and fish, in either pint or quart glass jars. The canned food supplied many meals for us throughout the years.

Summer, when the crops were ready for processing, was always hot and muggy. The basement was roomy enough for tables and buckets and boxes of fruits and vegetables.

The canning process was simple. First, the glass jars were scalded in boiling water and placed on the paper covered table. Then, Mother and her helpers would prepare the produce by cleaning, peeling, slicing, cutting or stringing each item. Each jar that was filled with fruit also got hot sugar water. Each jar that was filled with the prepared vegetables, got hot salty water poured into the jar. The heavy blue canner, with the metal divider inside, had been on the stove waiting for the water to boil. This canner sealed the jars. Mother just seemed to know how long to process whatever was in the jars. When that time was up, out came the heavy holders and each jar was carefully removed.

"Because the jars are hot, you must be sure not to touch anything as you put each jar on the table to cool," she instructed us.

This process was repeated many times over the years. As the preparations all happened away from

Eleanor with Charlotte, Paul with Lois

the kitchen, our family was able to go about our regular routine. I've seen many homes where everything was disrupted because: "It is canning season!" and the only wood stove was in the kitchen.

On November 16, 1934 our baby sister was born and named Marlene Irma. We prepared the room next to the kitchen for her until she grew big enough to have a bed upstairs with us.

Paul and Eleanor purchased their first car for $600. It was a Dodge 1933 model sedan and they bought it on April 10, 1935. Paul's beloved mother had been ill and died in 1936. She had been born in Germany in 1869. These were busy days for our family; Mother at home with us and Daddy working all day at the Schwab Commission Company warehouse. Sometimes we would go along in the car when Daddy went out to the farms to inspect the harvest.

Anna Mary's funeral. She died March 29, 1936.

He needed to know how much room would be needed in the warehouse for storage. As little girls, we would chatter all the way to the farm house. While the men talked business, the farmer's wives would serve us milk and freshly baked cookies. We always enjoyed our special time together with Daddy and he always talked to us as if we were older then we were.

He also spent many evenings at the firehouse or fighting fires that had started at the old farm buildings in the communities surrounding Mt. Angel. The young men of the town were all volunteer firemen and Daddy had many friends.

At this time, the local doctor made his medical rounds at the homes of his patients. We needed him at times, too.

Our need came on January 31, 1938, when the doctor said that Lois and I should be taken to the hospital in Silverton to have our tonsils and adenoids removed. I suppose our parents took us in the car because ambulances were used only in emergencies. Our parents paid the hospital $60.00.

Our father was always fascinated by every airplane that flew over our home. We would all run out of the house to look up at the sky to see the plane flying so high above us. Our home was fifty miles from the closest large airport in Portland. I don't know how my dad knew that there would be an airplane landing in Silverton in an empty field on April 24, 1938 and that the pilot would take anyone who wanted to go for a ride with him. But he did. Maybe an ad in the paper? Maybe his friends told him? We were so excited when he told us that we could see an airplane up close.

Daddy drove our car, with Mother, Lois, and baby Marlene, and me from the road onto the bumpy field a little way from the plane and stopped the car. Daddy said that if we wanted to go up with the pilot for a little ride we could. Both Lois and I said we would like to go, so Daddy walked us to the plane and the pilot helped us in the open door.

The plane drove over the bumpy field and we took off into the sky. We were seated close to a window so we both looked out to see the blue sky, a few clouds, and the scenery down below. He flew over Silverton and toward Mt. Angel, turned around and came back to the field and landed. It was an experience that we never forgot and talked about many times over the years. Apparently, something was said about Mother also going along, but Daddy told the pilot that Mother could not go. (She was pregnant.)

Lessons Learned

One late afternoon in Spring, when I was six and Lois was four, a storm was approaching our little town. The sky suddenly became very dark and the wind blew the rain sideways. Thunder crashed loudly, and lightning bolts lit up the sky and the inside of our house. We were crying and very frightened. Our dad took us out to the porch and gently told us that we would be alright. He explained all about storms and how the thunder and lightning are related to what was happening all around us. This must have allayed any fears that I might have had for all my life, because since then I've always been fascinated by storms.

One day in June, when Lois and I were ten and eight, we learned another lesson. Daddy had mowed the lawn and was complaining about all the weeds. He said that since our front lawn was the neighborhood playground that the grass would grow better for us to play on if the weeds were gone. So, all the children, cousins, friends, and neighbors, were asked to help.

He gave each of us an old kitchen knife and showed us how to dig out the weeds. He taught us how to work together to complete a job that was too big for an individual. The reward: a ride in the pickup to the next town five miles away to get firecrackers for all of us.

We really enjoyed that Fourth of July. We could hardly wait for nighttime to come so we could light up our hard worked-for treasures.

We must have been seven and five when we got our first bicycles. Since there weren't training wheels in those days to help teach you how to ride or to help a child balance, I learned how to ride when Daddy held onto the back of the seat. I pedaled and tried to balance at the same time as he ran alongside me. Then, when he knew I would be alright, he would stop running and let me go. I fell and tried again and fell and tried again as I was determined to learn. After many

Charlotte and her bicycle

tears and scraped knees and arms, my younger sister learned to ride her bicycle before I learned to ride mine.

A Big Change

A big change came into our family when I was nine years old. As the oldest daughter I had been admonished many times, "Charlotte take care of your sisters."

Now our parents had a BOY. Wow, the excitement in the house exploded. Daddy told us that he needed to get a box of cigars. The reason was explained as the necessity to announce the new baby by giving cigars to all his friends.

That didn't make sense to a 9-year-old girl!!

Invitations to family and friends to see the baby would be extended later when Mother felt better. Mother and Ron were in the hospital the required two weeks and when Mother came home with Ronnie, she was very weak. Next to the kitchen was a small coat/storage room with a sofa that we slept on when we were sick or recovering from a communicable disease.

Mother spent her days and nights in that room with the baby. The bassinette was kept close so she didn't have to move very far to nurse the baby. Mother told me how to support the baby's head and small body when I picked him up. I helped during the baby's waking times by following her instructions.

Since Ron was born in the spring, my sister and I had had to go to school which was about 4 blocks from our home. During the day, a hired girl came to do the house work and help Mother. But after school, we could help.

Taking care of children was something that I had done since I had turned nine. We lived close to many friends and cousins who were having babies, so I was always available to babysit even that young. But only for a short period of time. The mothers showed me what to do and, as the youngsters knew I was responsible for them, they did fine. Of course, I always had someone I could call if I needed help, but I never did.

The only one who gave me a hard time was Lois, my middle sister. She was always bossy and questioned everything I said.

When Mother felt stronger, I still helped with the baby as she needed.

We must have spoiled little Ronnie, because I remember sitting by his crib in his bedroom, waiting for him to fall asleep. I was told to wait right there until he fell asleep and then I could go to the movie with my friends. They were outside waiting for me, and I was eager to go. I would think he had finally fallen asleep, so I started leaving the room and he would scream for attention. I remember being very exasperated and kept putting him down in the crib and putting his blanket on him.

Our Town

The freight train moved slowly through town every afternoon. During the depression years, the flat-bed cars brought unemployed men who had hitched a ride on the slowly moving trains. If they were hungry, they would jump off the train car and walk to a house nearby the tracks. When Mother would see one of these men, she would call us in from playing outside and tell us to find something to do in the house. Then she would answer the door and tell the man that she would have a sandwich for him if he would sit outside on the porch. In addition to a sandwich, she would give them something to drink. The men always left after they had eaten. Many times they would ask if Mother needed anything done in return for the very appreciated meal. She always thanked them for their offers and they would leave to catch the next train.

A paved road next to the rail lines divided our little town. The bank, hotel, drug store, bakery and hardware store were on one side of the street and the railroad station, gas station, homes and the Fred Schwab Commission Company were on the other side. This was our downtown.

The paved road off the main street to our homes came up a small hill and our rocky road veered down the side of the hill. Our house was across the gravel road from the home of cousin Larry and his parents, Uncle Leo and Aunt Lauretta (Clouse) Schwab. They were next door to cousins Carol, Judy, Ken and their parents, Uncle Joe and Aunt Rose (Schwab) Wachter.

The walkway, next to the rocky road, was made of wooden planks that were laid like railroad ties with a space between each plank.

At the top of the walkway was The White Corner [named from its white exterior] Store. It was our grocery/variety store. As I was the oldest, Mother would give me a handwritten list of some things she needed. Everybody charged whatever they needed and at the end of the month paid their bill. No bills were ever sent. Since the owners of the store were my aunt's cousins, they always trusted me and I was always treated very nicely.

White Corner Store still stands at the corner of South Oak and East College Street. It now sells antiques and is open only three days a week: Friday, Saturday, and Sunday.

On my way along the wooden walkway, I would often find coins between the slats; mainly pennies. Once in a while, a nickel would be there and rarely a dime. It was so exciting walking along there and finding such treasures. I would come home and tell Mother what I had found. She said it belonged to me because I had helped her out by getting what she needed. Years later it occurred to me that Daddy had been dropping the coins down there. He so enjoyed teasing everyone. I can only imagine how he laughed when Mother told him my story.

All the children in the neighborhood were disappointed the year the boardwalk was taken out and cement became our sidewalk to the store. Especially me.

The stately Catholic Church had been built at the top of the small hill. The bells in the steeple would ring every fifteen

PARISH CHURCH MT ANGEL OR. 190

minutes. At each hour, the clanging would ring the time of day or night. Everyone would count the clangs of the bells. When a very old parishioner died, the bells' clang seemed to be endless to a young girl. We learned very young to sleep through the bells and even during the days we were not aware of the sound.

The church was damaged by an earthquake

that came through some few years ago [1993] and after restoration, the bell tower is back to ringing, doing its job.

Modern day St. Mary's

Last year I met the gentleman who is now pulling the long rope. He explained that he wouldn't be able to do his job very much longer as the tall, winding flight of steps was getting to be too much for him.

I wonder how many men have climbed those stairs to continue the tradition of the bells over the more than 100 years that the church has stood there so majestically.

On March 25, 1993, at 5:34 a.m., an earthquake with the magnitude of 5.6 on the Richter scale shook for 45 seconds. Its epicenter was Scotts Mills, Oregon and was felt as far north as Seattle, Washington and as far south as Roseburg, Oregon. People called it the "Spring Break Quake." The state capitol building in Salem, Molalla High School, and the Catholic Church in Mt. Angel, Oregon, among many, many other buildings, suffered terrible damage. The bell tower in St. Mary's Catholic Church in Mt. Angel, Oregon had to be restored after the quake. *

The Woods

Our home was built next to a grove of trees. The evergreens grew tall and stately. The deciduous were shorter and every autumn their falling leaves covered the floor of the small forest. "The Woods" as everyone called it, was a two to three block rectangle of trees. In the winter, the trees were covered with snow or ice and the blowing winds created movement throughout the hibernating landscape. In spring and summer, the budding trees and the wildflowers brought life and color back to The Woods.

We had many cousins who lived within walking distance of the forested area and we played there frequently. One summer day, the trees and underbrush were exceptionally dense. For some reason, there were unfamiliar sounds in the forest that frightened my cousin Maxine and me. We were curious, as two six-year-old girls can be, as to where the sounds could be coming from. What could it be? Should we leave the forest, or would we be safer staying where we were? Perhaps someone was waiting for us when we left our hiding place?

Then I remembered something and said, "There's no reason to be afraid. I have a pack of Lifesavers in my pocket. If they save lives, they'll save ours. All we have to do is put a Lifesaver candy in our mouths, keep it there, and we can leave safely."

We did and we were (safe that is).

The Schwab girls: Marlene, Lois, and Charlotte. 1936/37

Grade School Classes
First to Sixth

Our school was directly across the street from church. The school was named St. Mary's School and grades one through three were taught by Benedictine Sisters from the local convent. The teachers who taught grades four through eight were local graduates of the Normal School.

Going to school was exciting for me as four other cousins would be in my class. I also knew many of the other first graders as they were neighbors and we played together.

Since I lived close to the school I went home for lunch. Daddy worked close by so sometimes he would join us. He loved hearing my stories about what went on in school since I was a chatterbox. By first grade I had two little sisters in my family so we all had lunch together: Mother, Daddy, me, Lois, and Marlene.

In the fall, after all the farmers had their crops harvested and the warehouse work slowed down, Mother would tell us we were going to the beach. Daddy could get away from work and have some time with his family.

Lois, Marlene Paul, Charlotte
at Oregon beach cottage

The little cabin we stayed in at the beach had a main room for sleeping; a table for eating and playing cards, and a wood stove for heat and cooking. A small bathroom was in the corner.

We could hear the ocean over the hill. We found some steps to the beach and took off our shoes and socks and walked in the sand. Daddy always had funny things to tell us about the huge ocean and stories about the town and the beach and the stars and the moon. Our times at the beach were very special to our family as they were so rare.

When I was eight years old, I felt a terrible pain in my stomach and couldn't stand up straight. My parents called the doctor and he diagnosed appendicitis. I was taken immediately to the local hospital in Silverton, some six miles away. This was such a confusing time because it was dark, and I was scared. I cried because it hurt so much.

When we arrived at the hospital, I was taken into a white-walled room with lights so bright I had to shut my eyes. A mask was put over my nose and I smelled a terrible odor.

That's all I remembered until I woke up in a comfortable bed feeling like I was going to be sick to my stomach---and I was. Oh it was so awful!!!!!!!!!!!!!! I spent long days and nights in that bed. Very kind ladies in white dresses came to see how I was doing and they wrote on something as I told them what I was feeling.

After the pain was gone and the doctor explained what had happened, and that it was nothing I had done, I felt a lot better. When my parents brought me home, I still had to spend the next week on the couch in the room next to the kitchen. I was told I could walk to the bathroom down the hall, but I couldn't be too active. As I loved to read, that wasn't a problem. Classmates came by to keep me company and soon I was well enough to go back to school.

As one of the first German families who settled in Mt. Angel, we brought our Catholic religion and traditions with us. Because of this, the church and school were a major part of my early education. In addition to reading, writing, arithmetic, and geography, the Baltimore Catechism was our guide book to the morals and values that became a part of what we believe. Religion class taught us many stories from the Bible along with the historical significance of the Holy Land and other countries of the world. Many of our lessons included memorization, which was very difficult for me. I had to spend many days going over my memorization material before I could recite it.

A part of our Catholic faith included the sacraments. Our first sacrament was Baptism and then First Communion and Confession. The first-grade teachers taught the children about their Sacraments. The second graders spent their year preparing for their First Confession and their First Communion. It was a very exciting time for the children.

As the weather was usually sunny and warm in the spring, Mother's Day was set aside for us second-graders to receive First Communion. On the Friday before Mother's Day, we received our First Confession.

On First Communion Day all us little girls wore white cotton and lace dresses and the little boys wore white shirts and dark colored pants. We all were so excited to be able to receive Jesus's body and blood for the first time.

The following year on Corpus Christi Sunday in June, all us girls wore our pretty dresses again and carried baskets of rose petals. The day before, we had collected all the rose petals from all the rose bushes we could find in town and filled our baskets. Then on Sunday morning, we brought a basket and dropped the petals as we all followed the priest into church.

When the newly appointed Pope, Pope Pius XII, spoke to the world, we heard his message in English through the radio. Our teacher brought the radio into the classroom, so we could hear his message. Of course, we got poor reception that was full of static and his words were hard to understand, but someone on the radio told us what was happening in Rome and what the new pope was saying.

Confirmation was our last Sacrament [in grade school]. Our religion classes contained all we needed to know about the history of the church and Christ's messages through the epistles and the gospels. The Bishop of the Diocese administered the Sacrament of Confirmation and our teachers prepared us to know the answers to whatever question the Bishop might ask.

There were four of us with the same last name in the class, so we knew that one of us would be chosen by the bishop to answer a question. It could be any question relating to any part of our faith. It was nerve-wracking, and I hoped he wouldn't call on me. Luckily, he asked Jack who was very intelligent, made us look good, and I could quit shaking.

I learned an important lesson one school day in either fifth or sixth grade. All the girls in the class were friends and got along very well. One day, one of the girls said it would be fun if four of us would wear a red sweater and a brown skirt to school next Monday just for the fun of it. She mentioned our names. The next Monday, the four of us wore red sweaters and brown skirts. The teacher started the first class and at the end of class she called out our

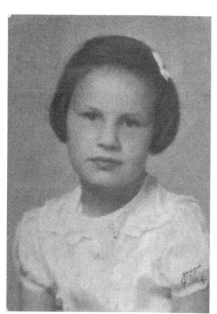

Charlotte. 1936/37

names and asked us to stay behind as she wanted to talk to us. Naïve Charlotte hadn't a clue about what we had done. The teacher said very kindly how nice we looked and then went on to ask us how we thought the other girls must have felt since we hadn't included them. I had not thought about them. This was a subtle message that I have never forgotten.

That method is just an example of the high-quality teachers we had in grade school. Miss Saalfeld and Miss Bauman were members of Mt. Angel families who had settled there early in the century and helped develop the town. Miss Keber and her family moved into town later but were just as responsible as the other families in stabilizing the town and farming community. Her brother was the president of the only bank in town. After she retired from teaching she was able to travel and develop the Senior Center in town. Miss Bauman's family established the telephone system for the community and to this day it is one of very few private phone companies remaining in the country. Miss Saalfeld retired and enjoyed golf at the local course and served on the board of several State of Oregon commissions.

The Room in Back of the Warehouse

The front of the warehouse had a loading dock with stairs on both ends. At the very top of the building was a distinguished sign with the name of the company; FRED SCHWAB COMMISSION COMPANY.

During harvest season, the building was filled with rows and rows of bulging sacks of seeds or grains or bales of hops piled high. The back of the long building contained another loading dock with railroad tracks below. This dock was used to load the railroad cars with customer's orders of seed sacks or bales of hops.

Daddy with his brothers:
Uncle Joe, Daddy (Paul), Uncle Fred who died soon after this picture was taken, Uncle Leo and Uncle Louis.
Picture taken in 1926.

The ceiling in the warehouse was so high, and the building was so big, that it was cool inside even on hot summer days.

As we had many cousins, we played with all of them constantly. When the warehouse wasn't full, we could play "tag" or "hide and seek" or "red rover" or any other game that we could think of.

The only thing we were warned about was "no climbing on the sacks or bales." The boy cousins and their friends would climb whenever they would not get caught. Otherwise, we were free to play as much as we wanted.

At harvest time, the farmer's trucks lined up in front of the warehouse (and down the dirt road) as they took turns unloading their crops that filled the sacks and bales. As each truck was emptied, the driver pulled around to the side of the building, parked the truck, and came in the door which was to the left of the front-loading dock.

The team in front of the warehouse:
Cousin Leo Meyer, Amanda (hidden), unknown man, Paul Schwab, Leo Schwab kneeling in front.

Inside was the company office. My older girl cousins, who had either completed their bookkeeping courses at high school or had been to business school, took care of all the duties there. The men teased the girls about boyfriends, a new dress or a new hairdo, while they signed their delivery statements.

My father or grandfather or one of the uncles stood down the hall from the office, welcoming each farmer/ harvester and inviting him into the backroom. It was not a large room, probably the size of someone's dining room. A long table was in the center of the room and wooden arm chairs surrounded the table on which were trays of empty glasses. On the walls were shelves filled with every kind of alcoholic beverage available.

I can only imagine how much alcohol was consumed just in that room alone. Oh, yes, this was hospitality in the late 30's after Prohibition.

Sons of Fred Schwab
Driver: Paul Schwab
Sitting: Fred Sch...

Our little town had two taverns and a small hotel with a lounge, where alcoholic beverages could be purchased. But the room in the back of the warehouse was where business dealings happened.

If the word "alcoholic" was known at this time I didn't hear it used. A man who could not hold his liquor was called a "drunkard." A woman who could not hold her liquor was called all kinds of things and admonished "she should know better."

The history of the use of liquor socially in Grandfather's family is unknown. Germany, from where our family migrated, is well known for their heavy consumption of beer. So, is it an inherited gene or does one's environment cause alcoholism? I often wonder about this and wonder how alcohol has influenced my family's medical issues. Grandfather became a diabetic, had to have everything he ate measured, and he died just after his 80th birthday. When I was twelve years old, my father developed pneumonia. He died at thirty-nine years of age, before penicillin, (which might have saved him) was completely tested in research laboratories. (My research has uncovered the fact that it was common at this time for alcoholics to die from pneumonia.) One uncle had consumed so much alcohol that his ability to speak clearly, and be understood, was lost for a number of years until he quit drinking completely. His wife and son took

Grandma Anna Mary and Grandpa Fred Schwab

him far away from the town where he had been born. He recuperated while working the night shift at a plywood mill. He outlived his wife and died in his 70's.

Another uncle never did get away from consuming alcohol. His wife, after several volunteer admissions to the state hospital, was able to stay away from alcohol herself, only after her husband died. In the next generation, at least one and possibly both of their sons had trouble with alcoholic beverages.

Both of my sisters married alcoholics (they didn't know it then). We are trying to inform our children about the family history of abusing alcohol, but we have so many unanswered questions ourselves.

Mother Had Two Aunts

Mother had two Aunts who lived in Mt. Angel. One lived in a red brick two-story house close to the grade school. The other lived on a big farm in the country about two miles from town.

Aunt Tillie's house in town had two cherry trees. Every July Lois and I would climb up the trunk onto a branch and eat all the cherries we could reach. No one could see us there because of the height of the tree and all the leaves on the branches. When anyone walked by, we dropped a few cherries. They would look up but apparently not see us. If I had climbed alone, I would sit up there and listen to the cars and people as they came by. It was so peaceful on a warm summer afternoon that I didn't want to come out of the tree.

To this day, some seventy years later, I can close my eyes and remember that innocent peaceful feeling of the seven-year-old little girl.

The Aunt in the country we called Auntie. Her name was Rose, and she was older then the Aunt Rose on the other side of the family. When we stayed at their farm, our bedroom was upstairs over the kitchen. After a cold night under the heavy blankets, we opened the floor register and welcomed the heat from the wood burning stove in the kitchen. Auntie was making breakfast. Uncle Cletus had been up since 4 a.m. milking the cows and he came in hungry and cold. We could hear them talking but they never talked about anything interesting to little girls.

When we went to the farm, either on our bikes or in a car with other adults, there were animals all over the yard; dogs, cats, chickens and often a cow or two. The smell was terrible. I must have had a very sensitive smelling system because no one else ever complained about the awful odor.

Eleanor Fisher Schwab, Marie Fisher holding child (probably her daughter Joan), Aunt Tillie, and Aunt Rose.

The Creamery

A cross the dirt road from Grandfather's house was the creamery. The cement building was U shaped with a loading dock on one side of the building. Each morning the truck drivers would unload large, heavy metal cans of milk onto the dock.

Mount Angel Creamery and Ice Company *

As children, we would watch but not get in the way. All the years we lived in town and played close by, we never went inside the creamery except for the buttermilk room. Its door was always invitingly open. Curls of dried buttermilk came out of a section of the machinery on the wall. The trick was to catch the curls with our fingers before they fell into a container below and become granules. The sweet taste of the curls of dried buttermilk was as enjoyable as an ice cream cone. Every time we would walk by and the door was open, we would enjoy the sweet treat. Also, every time we would walk by and the door was closed, we were disappointed.

The fathers of many of our friends and classmates worked at the creamery. They drove the trucks that collected the milk cans from the dairy farmers throughout the valley. Some of the men emptied the heavy milk cans into the separators. The cream was collected in a metal cylinder that had a spigot.

The creamery sold our community its supply of milk, cream, buttermilk, ice cream, butter, and ice. I was frequently sent, with 15 cents and an empty pint jar, to the retail area of the warehouse for a pint of cream.

But we—the Schwabs—didn't buy any butter.

We were sternly told not to say anything to our friends concerning butter. When one of the men in our family drove to Portland on family business, he would bring back packages for each of the Schwab families (his brothers and sisters). Inside the clear cellophane wrapped package was a white substance that looked like soft lard. It was called oleo. A capsule of golden coloring was included in every container.

My job was to break the capsule inside and gently press the soft substance between my fingers until all the oleo was a light-yellow color. Then it could be used. When the cellophane broke, it was a mess, nothing to do but put the oleo into a bowl and work the capsule into it with my fingers.

Oleo margarine is in common use today, marketed as margarine. It is sold low-fat or non-fat or any other way the advertising companies can make it appeal to the customer. Frankly, I still like the taste of butter best.

In the cash-strapped days of the Depression and during the butter shortages of World War II, margarine inexorably began to bypass butter. This was helped along by improvements in the manufacturing process—margarine was now made from hydrogenated vegetable oils rather than animal fats—and by a clever side-step of the yellow ban in which white margarine was sold with an included capsule of yellow food coloring. Buyers simply squished the two together to produce a nicely butter-colored non-butter spread. (Though not in Wisconsin, where using yellow margarine was a crime, punishable by fines or imprisonment.) Eleanor Roosevelt (in New York) promoted it, claiming that she ate margarine on her toast. *

Daddy in background working out piano bench so we can sit and all have picture taken together house in Mt angel smile for the camera Charlotte!

Charlotte's photo and her memory written to the right.

My Cousin Maxine

My grandparents lived in a house across from the Creamery. Their daughter Gertrude and her family had a house behind the Creamery, across from her parents.

Grandma had been born in Germany and Grandpa had been born in Dunlap, Iowa. I was very small when Gertrude died, so I did not know her. After much friction in the family, my grandparents (Fred and Anna Mary) adopted her children, Mary Jeanne, Maxine, and Ben.

Mary Jeanne was about five or six years older than I was, but I always remember how kind she

Maxine and Charlotte at Grandpa Schwab's funeral, 1943

was to me when I went to their house to visit with Maxine. When Grandpa was diagnosed with diabetes, Mary Jeanne had to weigh everything he ate.

Maxine was diagnosed with rheumatic fever when we were in grade school. The doctor said the treatment was bed rest for an undetermined length of time. A bed was put in the front parlor for her so the parlor furniture had to be pushed to one side of the room. The drapes that covered her windows night and day, and the carpet that covered the wooden floor, were dark and dreary. The only light Maxine got was from a small light by her bed. The room was gloomy but because of its location in the house, it was warm in the winter and cool in

At Paul and Eleanor's Home
Top row: Rose Schafer (friend of Leo Myer, Leo Mayer next to his mother, Josephine Mayer, Anna Mary Schwab, Anna Mary's brother Martin Mayer or maybe Paul Mayer
Bottom row: Charlotte, Lois, Amanda, Maxine sucking her thumb, Mary Jeanne, Ben Schwab.

the summer. Plus, it was the most convenient place for her classmates to visit her and for someone to take care of her.

As my home was a block (the short cut) away from our grandparent's house, I spent some time each day with Maxine. We played games, read stories, and played with our dolls, among other quiet activities.

At this time, the school district did not help bedridden students with their class assignments. Therefore, when Maxine's doctor said she was ready to return to school, she was two years behind her classmates.

We were told that the rheumatic fever permanently damaged her heart. Or did it? Maxine had gone through a lot in her young life. How can a gentle soul survive the death of her mother, being raised by austere grandparents, losing her home when grandfather died, being sent to boarding school, and marrying too young without it all affecting her? The only selfless love Maxine ever received was from her sister, her brother, and her three daughters.

> The Mayo Clinic defines Rheumatic Fever as an inflammatory disease that can develop as a complication of inadequately treated strep throat or scarlet fever. Strep throat and scarlet fever are caused by an infection with streptococcus bacteria. Scarlet Fever was a leading cause of death in children in the early 20th century. *

Finally, it was determined that her damaged heart needed to be repaired. Lois and I visited Cousin Maxine about a week before her surgery. She gave me a dime and said that she had taken a dime from our house when we were all little. She didn't want to die without paying back all her debts.

We teased her about the interest and predicted she'd recover and her heart would be ever so much better. Her premonition was correct. The surgery was not able to repair her damaged heart.

(Maxine died May, 13, 1975)

From left: Nick Michael, Aunt Tillie Michael, Gilbert Michael, Cletus Butsch, Florentine Michael, Aunt Rose Hassing, Cousin Louann, Ray Fisher, Marie Fisher, Bobbie Michael, Mother. In front: Paul Schwab holding Marlene, Charlotte, Lois, Jim Busch

Some Fisher Family pictures

Cousin Dorothy

Seventeen months after I was born, the time came for Mother to deliver Lois. My parents took me to stay with their good friends/cousins Uncle Fred J. and Aunt Bertha Schwab. They lived on a farm several miles outside of town and their oldest daughter, Dorothy, looked after me. She was fifteen years old and had two brothers. She had fun pretending that I was her little sister and playing with me.

Some years later when I was 15 years old and we had just moved to Salem after Daddy died, we received a phone call from Dorothy. She was almost due to deliver her third child and she needed help. Her regular help became ill and wouldn't recover in time, so she asked if I could come back to Mt. Angel and take care of her son, 4, and her 2-year-old daughter, for the two weeks that she would be in the hospital.

When I said, "Yes, I'd be glad to come," she asked me to come a few days early. If I came early she could show me the children's routine and they'd be more comfortable with me. She told me the day to arrive, so I checked on the bus schedule and packed my suitcase. After a warm, dusty bus ride, I arrived in Mt. Angel. The bus driver helped me with my suitcase and I walked the short two blocks to their home. Ralph, 4, and Mary Jean, 2, were charming, happy children and we enjoyed meeting each other.

Dorothy showed me the washing machine and where to hang the clothes to dry. It was the first time that I had seen a rotary clothesline. Then we went inside the house and I learned about the schedules: mealtimes, bedtime, and playtime.

After Dorothy and Sylvester left for the hospital, the schedules went smoothly. Occasionally, Dorothy's brother, Art, would stop by to visit and check on things. Dorothy's husband, Sly, would come to play with the children on his way to visit Dorothy at the hospital and to say good night before bedtime.

Once Dorothy came home and felt strong enough to manage the family, I took the bus back to Salem. When their baby girl was baptized, they named her 'Lois' which is my sister's name.

Schwabs: Charlotte, Mary Jean (Zodross) Joan (Dummer), Dorothy (Hammer), Rosemary (Hammer), Marge (Schmitt) Dorothy (Schmitt)

Trip to Alaska

Mother frequently wrote letters to her parents in Alaska. The only other way to send messages was by Western Union and that method was only used in emergencies.

When Ronnie was over a year old, Grandmother asked Mother to come to Alaska and bring all four of us children. Mother asked one of her cousins, Louann Hassing, to accompany us and help take care of us on the trip.

All the arrangements were made. We took the train from Portland, Oregon to Vancouver, British Columbia and spent the night at a hotel close to where the ships docked. Our adventure had begun.

The next morning, we took a hotel car to the ship and excitedly walked up the gangplank. We were shown to our rooms on the ship.

Cousin Louann slept in one room with us, Lois age 9, and I was 11. Mother shared her room with the two youngest, Marlene age 6 and Ron was a busy one-year-old.

Our meals were shared with the other passengers in the dining rooms. After dinner we went back to our rooms. We went to sleep listening to the music from the entertainment.

One night on deck, the bagpipe music blared through the door. It seemed very noisy since it was the first time I had ever heard bagpipes. Mother said that they played all evening and she enjoyed their performance.

The ship passed north through the Strait of Georgia on the eastern border of Vancouver Island. As children, we enjoyed watching the glaciers and rugged mountains along the shoreline. Ice fell off the jagged mountains and plunged into the water below. All kinds of sea birds

Frank Fisher

were flying over the ship. Each time we stood on the deck, the scenery had changed as we came closer to our destination. We brought books to read and toys to play with to occupy our time. There always seemed to be something going on that kept us busy on-board.

The ship stopped in towns along the way and delivered food and mail. Crew members carefully helped the passengers maneuver the gangplank, so

Fisher home in Hyder

they could debark the ship. Once we got to our destination, the ship turned into an inlet canal. We watched from the deck and were told by one of the ship's officer's that we "would be there soon."

Verona and Frank Fisher with their foster child Tom Jabrow

We finally reached Hyder, Alaska. Our grandparents and other friends of Mother's welcomed us as the ship arrived in port. Grandfather put the luggage and a few of us in his car and we drove to their home. Mother and Ronnie went with one of her friends. We all met at Grandmother and Grandfather Fisher's home.

After we were settled in for a few days, Grandmother told us that we were invited to meet the community of Hyder for a luncheon at "The Lodge."

The homes in Hyder (and other small Alaskan towns) had been built to withstand the fierce winds and winter snow. Thus, they were not large residences. So, all community celebrations were

A winter scene with Grandma Verona Fisher

held at The Lodge which was a two-story wooden building at the end of an unpaved road outside of town.

Grandmother's friends had planned a potluck luncheon, so we could meet everyone. Their delicacies included the

Hyder, Alaska winter in the 1940s.

tender meat of venison and moose plus salmon from the local rivers. The other treats that completed the meal were made from each family's special recipes.

After the lunch, a cousin told Lois and I that there was a glacier close by and we could see it if we wanted to go along with the other cousins. As we had never seen a glacier or even heard of one until this trip, we were excited to see what it looked like.

This was just the beginning of our explorations in Alaska.

Grandmother and Grandfather's house in summer flowers.

Verona Fisher enjoying the Alaskan heat

Hyder, Alaska
July 1940

Mr. and Mrs. Frank Fisher will be entertaining family guests this month, their daughter, Mrs. Paul Schwab and children Charlotte, Lois, Marlene and toddler Ronald. Accompanying them will be Louann Hassing, niece of Mrs. Fisher. They traveled from Mt Angel, Oregon.

The Fisher family's community of friends are eager to welcome the newcomers with a potluck luncheon at the Lodge, a visit to the glacier and then introduce them to the blueberry picking in the hills behind the town.

After the local newspaper's kind greeting to their visitors, everyone in the village welcomed the children with a friendly "hello there" as they explored the library and the ice cream store.

Soon, Grandma told us that the blueberries were ready to pick. Mother said that if Lois and I would get the pails from the back door and pick them full, she would make a blueberry

Grandma Fisher is on the right. She is with the neighbor ladies

pie. As we had loved any kind of pie she ever made, we decided to try to fill the pails. The only caution was that if we saw a bear, not to run since they move faster than we could.

Grandma told us, "Just drop on your knees and roll your body into a ball and the bear will go away."

When we had our pails full, we took them back to Grandma's house and Lois asked Mother how much we would get paid for two pails full of blueberries.

Mother paused and said "Girls, how much do you think we should then charge you for a piece of pie?"

Nothing more was said. We got the message and

Sitting on porch between 2 poles: Marlene, Charlotte behind her. Lois next to Charlotte. Grandfather standing on porch. Grandma with hat on standing beside Grandpa. Cousin with arms around them.

enjoyed a fresh piece of our first blueberry pie. To this day, we remember the lesson our school teacher Mother lesson taught us about generosity.

Festivals

Some of the small towns in the Willamette Valley had celebrations at harvest time. Hubbard had a hop festival parade and weekend celebration. Salem celebrated the cherry harvest; the community had a big parade and the Cherrians marched in their white suits decorated with cherries.

The largest city in Oregon is Portland and their celebration occurs in the spring when the roses are blooming abundantly and their organization that marches so proudly in the parade are called the Rosarians.

Children in the flax festival celebrating a community of cultures.

Our little town of Mt. Angel celebrated with the flax festival. That was always an exciting time for the children as the carnival came to town with the Ferris wheel and the merry-go-round that had multi-colored wooden horses. Many of these horses had been carved and painted by gifted artisans.

Another ride we liked were the small cars painted like automobiles that adults drove.

The most exciting event for us children was to ride on the float sponsored by our grandfather's feed and seed warehouse. Our mothers, aunts, and neighbor ladies worked diligently to fashion crepe paper dresses onto each of us. Then they taught us the "princess" wave. We all showed off our dresses which stayed on as long as we sat there. The farmer's flatbed trucks were used for the floats that had been decorated by its sponsor. Each float had a different theme that included bunches of golden flax around the bed of the truck.

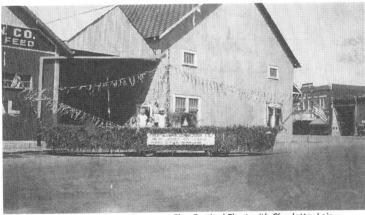

The Fred Schwab Commission Company Flax Festival Float with Charlotte, Lois, Marlene, and cousin Larry Schwab on the float.

The parade route was not very long because the town was not very big. The musicians of the "Oompah" band led the parade away from the main street for four blocks and then turned around and came back the same route. To us little girls it was a long parade.

The Flax Festival became the present day "Oktoberfest" which has grown over the years into a huge weekend event.

Disaster Hits

World War II was declared on December 7, 1941. The shipyards in Portland announced that they needed as many people as possible to build the ships that had just been ordered. Many young ladies just out of high school in our county went to Portland to see if they could be hired. At the same time many of the young men went to the recruiting stations to join one service or another.

There were so many questions: where was Pearl Harbor? What can I do to help my country? As youngsters in our grade school, we collected metal cans, took both ends off the cans and smashed them and put them in a gunny sack to be taken wherever they were taken. Apparently, the metal could be used again. Everyone willingly did whatever they could do. At this time, accordingly to the news my parents heard, England had a program to send their children to Canada. England had many air attacks from German bombers that continued every day and night all over their country and they were worried about their children being safe.

We found out that the United States was also considered a haven for the children. I overheard my Mother and Father discuss whether they should volunteer to be one of the homes because we had enough room for more children.

As an eleven-year-old who had always wanted an older brother, the offer sure appealed to me. Of course, my plan was never voiced, and I didn't hear any more of the program.

Charlotte with little Ron in the foreground. "I want my picture taken, too!" 1941

Any knowledge we received of the horror of what the Jewish people, the gypsies and others, were experiencing all came to us through the news reels. Those news reels played before each of the Western-type movies at our theater that was in the grade school auditorium.

Daddy's mother had been born in Germany and had died in 1936 in Oregon. She had many relatives who had stayed in Germany when she came to the United States about the year 1890. She would get letters from her sisters in Germany and would take off the stamp to find a short message about what their conditions were. One I was told about said, "This is awful." I remember that the conversations of aunts and uncles worrying about what was happening were animated with concern.

That was the atmosphere in our homes as December 1941 ended and January 1942 came.

Civil Defense
Air Raid Warden

When the Japanese bombed Pearl Harbor on December 7, 1941, the Civil Defense Department of the State of Oregon went into immediate alert.

The men of the town of Mt. Angel erected a lookout tower with wooden steps up to a wooden planked floor. The walls on two sides of the room were solid 2 by 4 lumber. The third side had a huge window opening for viewing the skies. The fourth side, where the steps entered the floor, contained a large doorway. On the walls were large posters with the silhouette and numbered types of every airplane ever made, both American and Japanese.

Since the West Coast of the United States was within flying distance from an aircraft carrier off the coast, an air raid warden was an important member of the Civil Defense group assembled to keep all the communities in Oregon on the alert. Each town had a similar tower and program.

On Saturdays around 2:00 or 3:00 p.m., Mother would take 3-year-old Ronnie with his favorite toys, something to eat for later in case they were hungry and walk down the gravel road outside of town to the tower. The tower was monitored for 24 hours.

What Eleanor carried when she kept watch over the skies.

American Red Cross Blood Donor Certificates

Many people in the country and our town were convinced that a strike would eventually hit the mainland. It had already happened in Hawaii, why wouldn't it happen in Oregon?

Mother felt like it was her pleasure and responsibility as an American citizen to protect her family this way. When she saw an airplane in the sky she would look at its underbelly and compare it to the poster hanging on the wall.

However, there were many days that Mother would tell us she hadn't seen any planes at all while she watched the skies.

Later in the afternoon, I walked to the tower in the field to bring Ronnie back home.

Before his bedtime, we had a sandwich and milk. Often, after another volunteer came to relieve her, Mother walked safely home in the dark.

Our Own Disaster

Our family had our own disaster hit us. On February 9, 1942 Father died suddenly. He was 39 years old and was diagnosed with pneumonia. Mother was 36 years old and they had been married for only 13 years. Our brother, Ron, would turn 3 in April, my little sister, Marlene, was 8 years old, Lois was 10, and I was 12.

Paul had been taken by ambulance to the hospital in Portland as the small hospital just 10 miles away could not help him. He was just too sick and needed more advanced care.

The next day, Mother took us girls aside into the living room and we sat together on the couch. She explained that Daddy had been very sick and had died. He would want her to tell us that he loved us very much and he was now in Heaven and would take care of us from there. We were stunned and probably in shock as we couldn't speak when she asked us if we had any questions. What could we say? She had explained it so gently.

She went on to tell us that for the next few days there would be many adults around who would be coming to visit.

Well! We had always had many adults around as our parents entertained their many friends and new acquaintances frequently. After she explained further what would be happening, she said we would be going shopping for clothes to wear to Daddy's funeral.

I remember clearly how composed she was and her demeanor made us feel calm. We spent that night at Auntie's home on the farm. [Aunt Rose and Uncle Jim Butsch]

The next day we went home to see Mother. A few of her friends were at the house helping her with arrangements. We answered the door bells as friends and neighbors came by bringing plates of desserts, casseroles to be refrigerated until baked, and boxes of goodies. The refrigerator on the back porch, the kitchen table, kitchen counters, and some card tables, were covered with plates of food. Aunt Tillie told us

Paul's wake. Eleanor sitting to the right. All the flowers were taken to the church for the funeral mass and then the graveside for the graveside service. Eleanor then gathered all the cards and placed them in a memory book.

this food was for the friends and relatives who would be coming in all through the night to pay respect to Paul at his "wake." A "wake" was a tradition of the German families who came to North America. The deceased would be in the casket at home, as we did for Daddy. People then came to pray and visit and eat and drink and share their memories.

The afternoon before the funeral, Mother took us into the living room of our home. Some of the furniture had been rearranged and the coffin was in the corner of the room.

Another view of the casket with Paul inside.

I remember going over to look at Daddy and he smiled at me. I have not told much about this time perhaps realizing it was so special.

That night we slept at Aunt Tillie's home a block away from our home.

The morning of the funeral, Mother sat us down and said, "Now girls, we will all act as young ladies." We knew that meant to behave ourselves as she had told us that many times. I remember it was a very confusing time and it was comforting to hear her speak with such composure.

St. Mary's Church was just a few blocks from our house, but Mother's brother, Leonard, drove us in his car anyway. Many people were standing outside, and we saw them as we got out of the car. We then walked up the many steps into the church.

There were colorful flowers around the altar and the lectern. All the lights in the church were on. The ushers guided us to where we were to sit: in the front row on the right side. It seemed like a long walk to the front rows where we had been many times before. Looking back, I see three little girls and one little boy who were totally bewildered. Our beloved Daddy was gone.

Archbishop Howard, with the other priests of the parish and priest friends of the family, said the funeral Mass. The church was crowded with relatives and many friends from around Oregon. Daddy was a volunteer fireman and active in the Knights of

Firemen friends at Paul's funeral.

Columbus organization and other organizations of business owners of Oregon, so he knew many, many people and was very well respected throughout the state.

After all the Catholic traditional funeral rituals, we left the church. I remember feeling so small going down that long aisle with everyone looking at me.

Once outside, we were ushered into the cars that had been waiting in front of the church. The casket was put into the hearse and we followed it to the cemetery.

I remember noticing that the grave was not far from Daddy's mother's and brother's gravesites. I also remember it was a sunny day in early February in Mt. Angel, Oregon.

Graveside with flowers from the wake.

After many prayers at the graveside, people milled about, and took pictures. I have pictures of Mother taken that day and they show a heartbroken young woman.

When some of the people got into their cars, the others followed, and the procession left the graveyard and headed for our house, as there was lunch waiting.

When we went into the house, Mother's friends were in the kitchen putting food on the tables. The main program for the afternoon seemed to be eating and visiting. Our aunt took us to her house so we didn't have to stay with all the adults. She had

Another view of Paul's graveside at Calvary Cemetery in Mt. Angel, Oregon.

planned some things to take our minds off what had happened if just for a little while.

It seemed strange to go back to school after all that happened. Since we had missed only three days, it seemed strange to return to something in our lives that had not changed.

Family members at Paul's funeral. Archbishop Howard is standing center next to Grandpa Schwab with Ron in front. Marlene and Lois standing in front of priest and Mother.

As a devoted Catholic, Paul would have received last rites (also known as extreme unction) in the hospital before he died. A person's "Last Rites" include penance, holy communion, and anointing of the sick. *

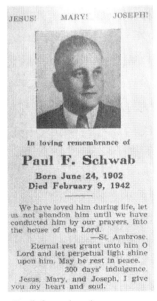

JESUS!   MARY!   JOSEPH!

In loving remembrance of

Paul F. Schwab

Born June 24, 1902
Died February 9, 1942

We have loved him during life, let us not abandon him until we have conducted him by our prayers, into the house of the Lord.
—St. Ambrose.
Eternal rest grant unto him O Lord and let perpetual light shine upon him. May he rest in peace.
300 days' indulgence.
Jesus, Mary, and Joseph, I give you my heart and soul.

Paul's funeral card.

Death Calls Prominent Young Business Man

Paul Schwab Died Monday Morning Following Three-Day Illness

ANSWERS LAST CALL

The untimely death of Mr. Paul F. Schwab at St. Vincent's hospital in Portland early Monday morning following an illness of three days which resulted in pneumonia shocked and saddened the entire community to the extent that individuals were asking themselves "Can it be true?"

Paul Schwab was born in Mt. Angel June 24, 1902, son of Mr. and Mrs. Fred Schwab, pioneers of Oregon and this community. It was here that he grew to young manhood, received his education in local schools. On November 28, 1928 he was united in marriage to Eleanor Fisher, and made their home here ever since, he being employed in his father's business, the Fred Schwab Commission Company, of which he was manager for the past 25 years.

PAUL SCHWAB

Pictured in the uniform cap of the Mt. Angel Fire Department, an organization he loved and worked for to make it the outstanding civic pride group of the community. He was chief of the department for many years, and still found plenty of time to take leadership in other community affairs, such as president of the Mt. Angel Business Men's Club and chairman of many other church and civic activities.

This article was saved in sections in Eleanor's memory book. It ran in the Mt. Angel News newspaper on Thursday, February 12, 1942.

Besides his wife, he is survived by four children, Charlotte, Lois, Marlene, and Ronald; his father Fred Schwab, sr.' eight brothers and sisters, Mary LeDoux, Rose Wachter, Amanda Wilde, Leo and Louis Schwab, all of Mt. Angel; Joseph and Mrs. Bertha Boylan, Stockton, and Mrs. Agnes Lindsey, Tracy, California.

Although only 39 years old, Mr. Schwab has spent many years in serving his community and his church. He was a member of the Mt. Angel Fire Department for the past 20 years, was its chief from 1930 to 1935. In 1939 he served as president of the Mt. Angel Business Men's Club and served on many of its important committees. He always took an active part in his church, when a small boy he served faithfully as an altar boy, later heading the annual parish festival, and when the parish needed a leader in the Archbishop's Confraternity of the Layety, Paul Schwab again volunteered and made it a success.

He was an active member of the Knights of Columbus, giving much of his time and money to aid the order in teaching the lessons on which the Knights are founded.

When a true friend, such as Paul Schwab has been to the writer, it makes one forget all principals of journalism, and just say the things in our own way as Paul would do when commenting on any of his friends or acquaintances. When the writer came to this community in 1934, Paul Schwab owed him nothing, but it was Paul who took him to his wide circle of friends, the splendid people of this community. In later years, when trying to thank him for these favors, Paul would just remark, that he only did what he would do for anyone coming to live in the community that he loved.

Paul, as thousands of people called him, was always congenial, never spoke harsh words about anyone, and even the few people who did not like him always admitted that Paul was always a gentleman in his dealings. He always gave his best in everything he undertook, and even with opposition (which everyone doing anything encounters) made it a success.

Thus in short we say, "Paul you have lived a short life, but in it you have given more than many who may live to, what is called the ripe old age, and we are among the many who hope that we may never forget you — and as you would say about your friend, "may he rest in Peace."

We wish to join the many friends in extending our sincere sympathy to his loving wife, adorable children, his venerable father, and the many relatives who were fortunate enough to have Paul as a brother.

All business houses were closed in Mt. Angel on Wednesday morning as the community attended the funeral services held from St. May's church at 8:15 o'clock.

Relatives, friends, and business associates from all over the valley were present at the Requiem High Mass celebrated by Father Alcuin. Also present in the sanctuary and assisting at the absolution were the Rev. Fathers James Koessler, rector of Mt. Angel college, Robert Keber representing St. Benedicts Abbey, and Hildebrand Melchior, assistant pastor of St. Mary's Rev. Father John Cummisky gave the funeral sermon,

choosing "You were so infinitely dear to me, so I drew you to me," as his subject. Graveside service was conducted by Father Alcuin, assisted by the State Chaplain of the Knights of Columbus Rev. Michel Raleigh of Canby, Rev. Fathers Robert and Hildebrand.

Members of the Mt. Angel Fire Department who acted as active pallbearers were Chief A. J. Butsch, Walter Smith, Joseph Wagner, Francis Schmidt, Alvin Saalfeld and Ben Traviss. The remaining firemen acted as ushers. Honorary pallbearers were officers of the Knights of Columbus E. B. Stolle, George Schmidt and Alexander Scharbach; and officers of the Business Men's club O. L. Withers, W. D. Harris ad Peter Gores.

Among relatives from out-of-town attending the funeral were: August Mayer, Tom Meyer, Richard Herald, R. and Mrs. Louis Schwab, Mr. and Mrs. Otto Schwab and Jeanne, Mr. and Mrs. Joseph Schwab, Mrs. Fred Niedermeyer and Roger, all of Portland. Judge Paul Fisher and son George, Mr. and Mrs. E. P. Scharbah all of Oregon City, Mr. and Mrs. Louis F. LeDoux, Marilyn and Jeanne, of Seaside, Mary Louise LeDoux, Salem. *

This gravestone, with only Paul's name on it, stayed as pictured for a brief time. Twelve years and 8 months later Eleanor's name joined Paul's.

Summer School

My memories are very fuzzy until the day Mother told us that she would need to make some money to pay the bills.

As she had been a teacher when she married, she told us that she planned to go to Monmouth where the college has classes she could take to bring her teaching certificate up to date. Grandmother Fisher was coming from Alaska to take Lois and Marlene to stay with her and Grandfather in Hyder. She went on to say that she would be getting a housekeeper who would stay in the house with Ronnie and me. As a responsible 12-year-old, I would be in charge of Ronnie. She would stay in Monmouth

> Western Oregon University was probably where mother attended college to bring her teaching certificate up to date. They still have a well-known College of Education. *

for the five days of school and then come home for each weekend. This schedule would continue all during her summer term.

It all happened just as she planned. Grandmother came down, took the two girls with her on the train to Vancouver, B.C., and took the next boat back to Hyder. Mother hired a housekeeper and I took care of Ronnie.

I have very little memory of that summer. It must have gone according to her plans or I would probably remember if anything unusual happened. We had many relatives on both sides of the family who lived close-by, so I always had someone to help me if I needed help.

After Summer School

After Mother came back from Monmouth with her teaching certificate up-to-date, she applied at our local grade school: St. Mary's.

She received her new teacher's contract on August 27, 1942. The fifth-grade class needed a teacher, so the school board hired Mother for that class. However, Lois was a fifth grader that year. Mother said it would be too hard on both of them to have Lois' Mother as her teacher, so Lois became a

Teaching in Mt. Angel: Mother, Miss Doalfeld, Miss Dehler, Fr. John Pastor of St. Mary's Church, Miss Berning, Miss Bauman, Miss Keber

student in the combined fifth and sixth grade class.

Each evening, Mother would have many papers to grade. With the regular housework that the hired girl couldn't get to because she was busy taking care of a very active three-going-on-four-year-old Ronnie, she had her hands full. But Lois and I would help her grade the papers when we could and do whatever housework she asked us to do. As the school year progressed, we could easily see that she was getting exhausted from all her hard work.

After our Father had died, Mother was invited to parties that were given by their mutual friends. One evening I noticed that she was not attending the parties anymore. I commented on the fact that she was home more evenings and asked what the problem was. Her reply surprised me: "It's a couple's world." After considering her answer, I realized that she was a very attractive woman about to have her 40th birthday without a husband to escort her.

Since Mt. Angel was such a small town, she didn't have many opportunities for employment, so she began considering other larger towns.

As her paternal uncle was a Court Judge in Oregon City, she spent some time researching a move there. That would have been an excellent place for us since Uncle Paul and his sister, Aunt Tillie had been living there for many years.

The only set-back that Mother found: there weren't any Catholic high schools in town. She wanted us to receive an education that consisted of the morals and values that she respected and was raised with. So, the next town she considered was Salem. Over the years, Mother had made friends through the organizations she had joined. Many of these friends lived in Salem. She treasured their friendship and their cardplaying abilities. Mother loved to play cards. So she set her sights on Salem.

Charlotte's High School Years

The summer after my eighth-grade graduation, Mother decided that my 9th grade year, the 1943-44 school year, would be our final year in Mt. Angel. We would be leaving a town where my father was born. Where I was born. Where my parents were married. Where the Schwab name was highly respected.

Written on the back: Graduation from Saint Mary's School. I'm in there somewhere with my new first permanent.

Charlotte's Elementary School Diploma. May 26, 1943. Chairmen Board of Directors was her Grandfather Fred

So, as I started high school at Mt. Angel Academy, she started to make plans.

The girls I had been going to grade school with also attended the Academy as did the girls from small towns close by. The Benedictine Sisters had been teaching students there from all over for many years. They came from other areas of the state and from out-of-state. Because so many families wanted a quality Catholic education for their children, they eventually started a boarding school. The student dormitories were on the third floor with classrooms on the second and fourth floors. I took piano lessons about two years in their piano room on the fourth floor. When my father died, we had to make some adjustments, so we needed to cut back on expenses. As Mother was an excellent pianist, she thought I would be also. She started my lessons, but I didn't do very well—although I really tried.

Next to the education building was the Convent building with offices, living facilities for the Sisters, and a chapel. All these buildings were constructed in the late 1800's and early 1900's. (Several years ago, the earthquake made it necessary to rebuild the old school building. The school gymnasium with the beautiful wooden floors and ceilings were saved and refurbished. This room is now the St. Agatha Room where Norm and I had our 50th anniversary reception and dinner [in 2001]. This room is used for meetings, dinners and wedding receptions.)

The gymnasium was a major place for school activities. I remember learning to march to the recordings of John Philip Sousa's marches. It was great training for the freshman class in listening and responding instantly as well as group organization.

Sister Carol knew we were moving to Salem and she knew where I would attend school once I was there. She took me aside and told me that the freshmen in Salem were learning Algebra and here we only had a general math class. She taught me Algebra privately that year in addition to my regular general math class. I don't learn any math easily, but I received enough education from Sr. Carol to be equal to my classmates in Salem.

John Philip Sousa's songs are extremely patriotic with songs like: The Stars and Stripes Forever and Semper Fidelis. During a time that the world was at war, these moments of American pride were important to keep up morale.
*

During my freshman year, the students gave monthly donations to be sent to the "pagan babies in Africa." I was recruited to be the treasurer for the donations. Usually people only gave pennies or nickels, so it was my job to collect them and keep an ongoing total.

In December, my paternal grandfather died, Fred Schwab.

Jesus!   Mary!   Joseph!

Enclose within Thy loving Heart, my Jesus, the souls of father and mother

Fred Schwab

Born at Dunlap, Iowa Nov. 1, 1863.
Died Dec. 8, 1943 at Mt. Angel, Ore.

Anna Mary Schwab

Born at Wuerttemberg, Germany Dec. 2, 1869.
Died March 29, 1936 at Mt. Angel, Oregon.

My Jesus Mercy!
Sweet Heart of Jesus be my love.
Sweet Heart of Mary be my salvation.
Most Merciful Jesus grant them eternal rest.

Fred's funeral card. Fred and Anna Mary: together in eternal rest.

He had diabetes for many years and his oldest daughter, Mary, had been caring for him. He was eighty years old when he died. His life had been busy and very productive. He was the first mayor of Mt. Angel. He had been interested in Oregon politics, and had many political friends who would come to visit. As a business owner, and ex-mayor, he knew many people around the state and his funeral was well attended.

Grandpa Fred Schwab died December 8, 1943. It was almost two years after my father, (his son) Paul, had died. Paul's death must have been very hard on him and took its toll.

Life Without Daddy

Mother went to the reading of Grandfather's will with the other members of the family. After the will was read, Mother's comment was, "I saw his will before, and this has been changed." From reports I was given by very reliable witnesses, Mother was very angry and let the family members in that room know it.

When Mother came home, she told me that the will had been changed and the four of us children would get a small sum for our future medical expenses, but that was it. She told me the amount, but I have forgotten. The hardest part of this experience for me was what it did to my mother. She was a widow of their most trusted son who had worked night and day for the company. Because we were basically written out of the will, Mother felt disrespected and dispossessed. She was very hurt by the way she was treated.

She said, "What goes around, comes around." I knew what she meant. She felt that the person responsible for the will's change would end up getting their comeuppance. Soon after, she told me a lawyer had told her that she had grounds to sue but she said, "No."

Life went on. School went on. Mother continued to make plans to move. She sold the car. She sold the house and purchased one in Salem at 630 N. Cottage St., so we could walk to our schools, she could walk to work, and we could all walk to church.

We moved to Salem in June with Uncle Leonard driving us there in his car. Ronnie cried, Lois and Marlene asked question after question about what the new location would be like. I remember being joyful and excited as we drove to our future home.

Eleanor on moving day 1944.

When we arrived, the moving truck driver and helpers unloaded our furniture. Mother then directed them where to put everything in the rooms downstairs, and bedrooms upstairs. By the end of the day, we were settled in our new home. It didn't seem very long until we met the neighbors and our daily routine became familiar.

Mother's job was at a downtown drugstore, the old-fashioned kind that had a soda fountain. Her work schedule were days and then evenings all week. Whatever she made, she indicated she did not make enough to cover all our expenses.

One day she said she was going to rent out the main floor bedroom. The servicemen were coming back from the war and attending Willamette University on the GI Bill. The dormitories had already been filled, so the downtown homeowners were asked to rent out rooms to accommodate the new students. Mother said she planned to rent to a male student. The room had a bathroom in the hall next to the bedroom and we were cautioned that we were to be fully dressed when we came downstairs from our bedrooms on the second floor.

Downtown drugstore, Wiles Drugstore, where Mother worked was next to the Grand Theater.

It didn't last very long because apparently our first boarder, a young man, had a female visitor at night that came in through the window. When I asked Mother where he was the next day, she said, "He hadn't acted appropriately." And that settled that.

Before I started school, I wondered what it would be like to go to Sacred Heart Academy in Salem without knowing anyone. As it turned out, one of my classmates had been in our grade school graduating class. He just happened to be a boy I had a crush on in sixth grade. Since I was coming from an all-girls school (Mt. Angel Academy), it would be quite different having boys in the classroom. The Academy was five blocks toward the State Capitol building from our house. It was an easy walk in any weather. St. Joseph's Church, the grade school, and the grade school playground were all on the same blocks as the Academy.

I was unfamiliar with the order of Holy Name nuns who would be our teachers, since I had grown up with the Benedictine Sisters in Mt. Angel. I soon learned that our teachers were experienced, well-educated, and well-traveled. They all knew the world first-hand as they taught us about geography, history, and the like.

As a sophomore and 15 years old, I felt like my world had really opened for me. I soon found out how different it was to go to school with boys. Some of them smoked and some begged smokes from them. There was a no-smoking policy in the school and on the school grounds. No problem!!!!! They smoked on the curbs next to the road. It was so funny to watch them try to look cool from inside the classrooms.

I didn't have a large class as most of the local high school students attended Salem High School on Capital Street. Our boys' basketball team played Salem High and no matter what high hopes we had of winning, the Salem High team was better and won every game.

Living in Salem

The next summer we planned to go berry picking. Salem had an excellent program set up for picking the crops. The school buses were used. A teacher, or a mother, oversaw the bus full of sleepy-eyed kids who were eager to make some money. Some were serious about making money and some were more serious about getting away from a parent for the

Lois, Charlotte, Marlene, Ron in front of the Salem house.

day. The person in charge of the bus had the authority to send any trouble-makers off the bus.

Strawberries were the first crop ready for harvesting. That first day I discovered that I was a terrible strawberry picker as I had to lean over or crawl on the ground to reach the crops. The sun was very hot and it made me sleepy and cranky. When we got back after the first day, I told Mother that there had to be something else I could do. As I was only 15 and the law said that I had to be 16 to work, I could not just work anywhere. The next day I inquired at the laundry/dry cleaner's business close-by. I would need my parent to sign that it was okay with her. She signed gladly, so I had the job.

I'm sure that it was the hottest summer Salem had ever seen. And inside the laundry were the washers, dryers, and ironers sending hot steam into the air. After I was taught the right way to use the mangle to iron the sheets and shirts, I was set for the summer. "There is a technique for everything," Was what I learned the summer of 1945. Oh, a nice cool shower felt so good after work when I got home. I remember wearing a flowery printed cotton dress every day and washing it every evening. It was steamy hot work, a great work experience, and the sun was not shining on me. I was so grateful.

During my junior year, we had to write research papers for some of our classes. Since our school was close to the Oregon State Library, we spent many days researching our topics and writing our conclusions.

Another interesting trip we made was to the Oregon State Prison. We saw the cells and an underground bunker which they used for solitary confinement. It wasn't any place any of us ever wanted to experience.

The only sports activities at school involved the boys who were interested in either football or basketball. As we did not have very many boys they could be seen participating in both sports.

The Candy Store

Immediately after school each day, I had to leave for home to take care of Ronnie so Mother could go to work. Usually, she started dinner and I saw that Ron, Marlene, and Lois were fed. We all cleaned up after dinner then did our homework and any other chores Mother had left on the list. Bedtimes were set and adhered to because we had to get up early every morning.

Eventually, Lois met some girls about her age who were interested in making money picking strawberries. She found out that a school bus, parked in a central location of the neighborhood, left early each morning and took the youngsters to the strawberry fields at the farms outside of Salem. They were paid for the number of boxes they filled each day. An adult, either a farmer's relative or a teacher, was in charge of each group on the bus. At this time, I worked at the laundry within walking distance of our home.

One Saturday, Mother told me that there was a candy store just down the street from the drug store where she worked. She told me that since sugar was rationed this business only received enough supplies to be open one day a week and if I would go to the candy store and buy a pound of chocolates for her she would give me a chocolate treat. Then, Mother said the reason she needed me to do this was because she doesn't like to stand in lines for anything!

She gave me the money and when I arrived at the store I knew exactly what she meant. The little shop was full of customers waiting for the business to open. I added myself to the group. Most of the customers were couples. Each person would be allotted the same: one pound of assorted chocolates.

Eleanor welcoming her new life.

We were each given a number when we entered the shop. There were empty display cases on three sides of the room. As people were busily visiting with each other, the conversations filled the room with stories and laughter. It seemed like finally the sales lady began to start bringing the filled paper sacks from the back room. As each number was called, the customer came forward for their pound of chocolates, smiled their thank you, and made their way to the door. This was an interesting experience for a fifteen-year-old girl who was doing a favor for her beloved Mother but also looking forward to her reward.

Junior Year

As high school juniors, we all worked on the Junior/Senior prom. Our main contribution was to make butterflies out of crepe paper. Strange, I am still enchanted with butterflies.

We spent our extra time before the prom finding partners to dance a dance with each of us. Usually several girls would back some boy in a corner and we would ask him which dance he would dance with each of us. We would then write his name in our dance book. It seems like there were 12 lines in our little booklet, one line for each song. We attached the booklet to a ribbon on our wrist. After each dance I would find the next boy on my list. It was great fun, causing lots of laughs.

After the prom, many of the couples who had double-dated, would get something to eat at a restaurant and then drive to the beach to see the sun come up.

That summer I worked in the soda fountain at the pharmacy. I heated up soups, made sandwiches, fixed soft drinks from the fountain and made milkshakes, sodas, and malts. The pharmacy was directly across the street from the Marion County Courthouse in downtown Salem. Hungry customers from the courthouse came for lunch every working day. I learned to take an order, get it ready, and serve the customer quickly. Of all the orders I took, a chocolate ice cream with caramel topping still makes my mouth water.

I was also continuing to babysit every chance I got and made enough money to buy some of my own clothes. I had planned to get an outfit or a dress, so I asked Mother if she could go shopping with

*Eleanor and Charlotte
630 N. Cottage St. Salem*

me. She said she had something else she had to do. I tried to

change her mind and said I needed her opinion on my selection. She said not to be concerned because if I did not like how it looked when I came home, I could always take it back. I didn't know I could do that! I had a very successful adventure, found exactly what I wanted, and I looked great in it.

Written on the back: So proud of my choice: pink and green plaid skirt with darker pink sweater.

Senior Year

When I registered for classes my senior year, it looked to me like I would have an extra period that I could use for study hall. Sister said that study hall was not an option and that I needed to pick a class to fill that period. The only one I could take was Spanish. What did I know about Spanish? I had already taken two years of Latin. Oh well!! OK. Spanish it is. Who would have known I would enjoy that class so much? What a beautiful language! The only mistake I made on the exams were forgetting to answer with the Spanish word instead of the Latin word. I did very well in the class and learned to admire the language.

Some of our classmates dated but the rest of us just went together to the movies and then to the ice cream shop afterwards. The family of one of our classmates owned that shop so we gathered there often.

When the nuns were all busy teaching, the principal would ask me to watch the front door of the school. One time I answered the door and a couple with their son asked to see the principal. I let Sister know that she had company and led them into the meeting room. The sound of their voices was magnified because of all the wood in that 3-story building, so I was able to hear their story, even without trying. Their son had been expelled from public school and they wanted to know if he could go to the Academy. Her answer was a definite NO. Then she escorted the family out the door.

My special friend at school was Sister Marian James, our chemistry teacher. Early in her teaching career, a beaker had exploded in the lab and hurt her eyes. The plastic surgeon that had done her surgery that long ago had done a very good job on the upper part of her face. As we looked at her, we couldn't tell what she had been through. My friends and I would sit on the lab tables after school and talk with her about many things. Sometimes, it was about what happened at school or she would share some information with us. She was fun to talk with because she always had kind suggestions and great advice that helped us.

Sister Cecilia Mary was our homeroom teacher and the girls always told her that she favored the boys. But she always said that we were all her favorites. I remember she seemed to want to prepare us for what we would encounter in the "outside world." I don't remember exactly what she said only that she earnestly needed to tell us.

In the spring, the juniors put on prom for us seniors. Some of the returning servicemen were coming back and wanted to finish their high school classes and graduate. One of them was from Salem and he had joined our class in September. I was excited when he asked me to go with him to the prom. He was tall, dark, handsome, and a very nice young man. We double-dated with Anna and Fred, classmates who were dating at that time. We all had a great time, stopped at the ice cream parlor for a treat after the dance, and then he saw me home.

Fred had his car at the school, so he took Anna home. The next day, Anna confided in me that she was going to attend Marylhurst College after we graduated and study to become a Holy Name Nun. I wasn't surprised as Anna's older sister was a Holy Name Nun. Anna said that when she told Fred after the prom he was very supportive of her vocation.

Our classmates have had many reunions together and several years ago Anna contacted us from Spokane, Washington. She said that after many years of teaching the harp, she had returned and would be living in Spokane.

As high school graduation came closer, it was time for the senior play. I remember it was fun practicing our parts. On one of the last days of practice, Sister said the play was cancelled. I remember feeling sad and I remember that they never gave a reason for the cancellation. Asking classmates didn't give me an answer. I was curious for many years until one of our class reunions. It could have been in Reno for the 50th reunion, I'm not sure. During the many conversations someone mentioned the senior play which caused much laughter. Naïve Charlotte again! I asked whatever happened that cancelled the play. It seems some of the classmates got a mischievous streak and property damage ensued. I don't remember what they did, but I do remember it was the same group that had gone to grade school together all those years ago. They were always coming up with one mischievous act or another. To this day they are still a happy bunch.

Many of our classmates have gone on to their just reward. There are not as many anymore who come to the reunions, but they are still around and every once in a while, someone comes up behind me and says, "Guess who?"

Over the years I've talked to many people about education. It makes me reflect on my own education and I feel very appreciative and grateful of my high-quality Catholic school education. I always had outstanding teachers and when I needed help with my assignments, I always got it. My grades throughout have been average and I had to study very diligently.

Charlotte After High School

The summer after high school graduation I worked at the soda fountain at Wiles Pharmacy as I had done the previous summer. I also babysat as much as I was needed.

The goal was to make as much money as I could. I was planning to start the program to become a nurse at Providence Hospital in Portland, Oregon. They had a three-year program to educate young women who were committed to becoming registered nurses.

As I had been planning this for my life's work, I arrived at the nurse's residence early. The letter I received indicated that we were to be at the location on 47th and Glisan between two and four o'clock. I arrived before two and the other students arrived about three. It was an excellent way to become acquainted with my new classmates one at a time.

The brick building in which we gathered was called the "baby home." Babies and small children with serious birth defects were cared for on the top floor. The main floor included offices, meeting rooms, a large entrance room and a small room, close to the front door for Johanna who was our house mother. When visitors came, or any packages were delivered, Johanna would notify us. We didn't know anything about Johanna only that she was there to monitor the front door and she carried out her role with a special kindness. Lights had to be turned off by 10 pm and everyone needed to be in bed. Johanna came through in the dark, checking us, and when she was off-duty one of the Sisters would come through.

I was assigned to share with seven other girls the only dormitory room that was in the basement. The other rooms were shared by three girls each.

Five of my roommates grew up in Portland. Carolyn Thorup was an only child. Her father was a doctor who was very active in the medical community. She bubbled with the joy of living and had many friends. She welcomed her classmates every August to their lovely home in Lake Oswego. She made lunch and served us outdoors in her backyard amid the flowers and shrubs that she and her helper had planted.

Anita Sherar, called Skeeter because it fit her better, had attended Reed College the year before. She then decided to see how she liked being a nurse. She loved jazz music and listened to it all the time. (This was my introduction to jazz and I am still fascinated by it.) We were all welcomed to her home and her parents encouraged us to write our names or draw a picture on the wall by the door. Someday they were going to paint it; just not yet.

Phyllis Weber had generous parents and four younger brothers who welcomed us anytime. Phyl developed mononucleosis and, while recuperating at the hospital, a spark was lit between Phyl and young Dr. Bill Fisher that ended in marriage. The Navy had paid for his medical education, so they were married at the base in California and spent a few years there. When they moved back, they purchased a home in Portland, close to Providence. Phyl graduated with the class of 1952, and Bill set up his medical practice in Portland and spent many years as a well-known physician and teacher.

Juretta Oliver was an excellent student and very intelligent. We called her Jerry as each one of us had to have a nickname. We would all go together when someone suggested walking to get a snack. This one day we decided to go to Yaw's in Hollywood for hamburgers. That district was a mile or more away, so we started out walking. As some had trailed behind, there were five of us that arrived first. We told the hostess how many were in our group, so we could get a table large enough for all of us. She looked at the few of us standing there and said we couldn't stay there. I could see they had tables for large groups, so I was confused why she would turn us away. I turned around to my friends to see if they knew why she had been so rude. It took me a few seconds to realize that she meant they wouldn't serve us because they didn't serve blacks. We left just as the others caught up with us. After explaining what had been said, Jerry said that was ok, she would just meet us later. Everyone agreed: you don't serve Jerry, you don't serve any of us. I often wonder how many times she was humiliated like that. This was 1948-49 and I had never seen anything like this. We spread the word and no one we knew ever went to what was regarded as the most popular restaurant in Portland.

After graduation, Jerry went on for her degree and joined a medical center in north Portland and, with other dedicated nurses, set up a program to serve the very poor and disadvantaged families who lived there.

June Dawn was a very strange young lady. We never knew if she was telling the truth. We never really got to know her. She said her real name was Veronica and she didn't like it, so she changed it to June Dawn. She was expelled early on for stealing.

Mary Ella Kelly was an only child from Missoula, Montana. On our first Thanksgiving together, her parents sent her a turkey dinner with all the trimmings. Somehow, with special deliver, it was still warm. We all had a great Thanksgiving dinner that year.

Marianne Krielich was another oldest daughter and she had three little brothers. She has always been artistic and is a quiet, gentle lady who now has a wonderful husband and family. One of her sons is a Catholic priest and two of their daughters are nurses.

Our entire first year was exciting; there was always something going on with this group. Skeeter didn't like a curfew because she never had one. I slept very soundly so I didn't know when she climbed out our window and came back in late. Oh, the stories she would tell!!

We were probationary students for the first months and called "probies" by the other students. We had to learn the essentials of patient care; how to make beds with and without the patient in the bed, how to take a temperature, how take blood pressure, and how to give shots. We also learned short cuts in charting and other patient protocol.

It was an exciting first year!

Memorial Day, May 30, 1948
Vanport Flood

As most of the patients had bedside radios turned on all day long, the news of the flood on the Columbia River spread fast. It was May 30, 1948, and the city of Vanport was flooding. A railroad dike had burst and high water from the Columbia River had flooded the entire town of Vanport, Oregon.

Vanport was an area on the south side of the Columbia River that had been hurriedly built for workers and their families. The workers had jobs in the shipyards and they and their families lived in buildings similar to army barracks. At that time, Vanport was the second largest city in Portland and predominately African American.

This flood destroyed many homes and took many lives. Fifteen people were killed, and 18,000 people were left homeless as the floodwaters destroyed the entire city. At the time, all we knew was that there was a flood north of town. Several nurses took the elevator to the hospital roof hoping they could see what was going on. Apparently, that didn't give them much satisfaction as they didn't have anything to share. I did talk to someone who had flown over in a small plane and reported he saw water all over.

This entire area is now North Portland and contains businesses, hotels, restaurants and also dog racing and car racing tracks and some very beautiful neighborhoods.

When I Met Norm

When we met for class that first day, the Superintendent of Nurse's training explained the rules of the program. Miss Leonard made it very clear that not all of us would be graduating in the three years it would take to prepare us for the State Boards and to become Registered Nurses.

The first six months we were Probies and eager for January so we could take care of patients in the hospital.

When summer came, we had a month off from classes. Plans had been made to build an addition to the hospital for student rooms. We would have only one roommate. Having shared the large dormitory for a year with seven other students, I looked forward to a new adventure.

I took the bus back to Salem with all my belongings; which were just books and clothes. After a month at home, I needed to get back to Portland. My classmate Shirley said her boyfriend had a car and could take us back.

Shirley's boyfriend brought his childhood friend along, so he would not have to drive the long distance back home alone. As we did not have any extra luggage, just our suitcases, we fit into the small car just fine. Dale and Shirley sat in front and we sat in back.

We covered many topics during the long drive to Portland and as Dale's friend had been out partying the night before, they decided we had better stop for a milkshake. As you can see, he didn't make much of an impression on me. He had black hair and brown eyes and was taller than me, but the hung-over look wasn't very appealing.

Norm at 18 years old

They treated us to a nice lunch when we reached Portland. Our next stop was St. Vincent's Hospital; in the hills of the northwestern part of town. A tall red-brick vine-covered building which would be our home for the next three months.

Our classes in OB/GYN included taking care of new mothers, delivering babies either naturally or by Cesarean and learning to appreciate the miracle of birth.

Male-type people were only allowed on the main floor of the nurse's residence, so we said our thank yous and goodbyes

Norm's high school graduation photo

and signaled for the elevator. My new friend said he would like to see me again and would I like to fly in a small plane with him. That sounded like fun, so he told me he could rent one at a small airport outside of Portland next time he came up. We could go together since he had a pilot's license. He asked me what my last name was, so I told him, "Schwab."

As I got in the elevator he said, "What a name, Charlotte Schwab."

I snapped back, "Well your name isn't any better."

Then, as he held the elevator door open, he said, "I'm going to marry you."

Talk about a line!

So, I said, "You're crazy, I am not getting married to anyone."

And then the elevator doors closed.

Rotation:
St. Vincent's Hospital
Obstetrics/Gynecology
June 6, 1949 to July 28, 1949

Since Providence Hospital was new, some of our classes were taught at St. Vincent's Hospital, where we joined their students in the classroom. My first rotation assignment was also scheduled there. The trolley transportation system had been established many years ago so our trip to St. V's was easy. We could get on the trolley at 47th and Glisan St. and get off on the other side of the river just in time for classes and our rotations.

When we were on night duty in the delivery room, and when our classes were in that same building, we stayed in the nurse's residence. The rooms were set up for two roommates.

We continued having classes and soon learned all the procedures necessary to take care of mothers and babies. We even taught new parents how to hold a baby and how to take good care of their newborn. At this time, mothers and babies stayed in the hospital for two weeks after the birth.

St. Vincent's Hospital. Portland, OR *

As the head nurse had been a classmate of Mother's cousin many years before, she took a liking to me and I assisted in many Cesarean Sections. What a thrill that was!!!! Many times, the birth was in the middle of the night. They all came when they were ready. This was my favorite rotation. It still amazes me how the progress of knowledge has brought so many changes in my lifetime and yet, a baby is still a wonderful celebration. We need to take special care of what God has created.

Rotation:
Pediatrics and Well Baby Home
September 5 to October 31, 1949

Both the Pediatrics area of the hospital and the Well Baby Home gave us experience with children who needed extra care. Each place provided a degree of care that the baby needed.

In the Well Baby Home, nurses took care of children with birth defects who were not ill but needed professional care. Their parents could visit them anytime they wanted.

Pediatrics took care of children who were ill and needed medical care. Parents could visit for one hour only.

One child has been a part of my memory for all these years. The nursing staff had been doing everything possible for this little boy who was in a coma. It was worrisome for everyone, even the doctors. He had been a patient for two weeks. The next morning when I came on duty, he was standing up in the crib, jumping around for attention. We learned a good lesson: NEVER GIVE UP!!!

Rotation: Psychiatry

Each student nurse was required to attend classes in psychiatry at the Oregon State Hospital in Salem. I spent the months of December 1949, and January and February 1950, with students from teaching hospitals in both Oregon and Idaho. We lived in the nurse's residence on the Oregon State Hospital grounds. The building where we lived, and a few other buildings, were newly built of red brick. The older buildings on the south side of Center Street are the original ones built many years ago. If you saw the movie "One Flew Over the Cuckoo's Nest" you saw the insides of those buildings. They were dark rooms that had heavy security screens on the inside and on the outside of the glass windows. The floors were made of wood and had been cleaned and bleached many times over the years.

Each ward had a communal sleeping area and each patient had a bed and dresser of their own. They ate their three meals every day in the community dining room.

The administration building contained a large room where the patients could attend weekly dances if they were certified ready for socializing. As students, we were expected to observe the interaction between the patients and encourage participation by introducing the shy men and women to each other.

At the beginning of December, a women's group from the town gathered together and drew up a plan to see that each patient would receive a gift for Christmas. The wrapped gifts had tags labeled for man or woman. In mid-December, I was one of the students who worked in the library delivering books and magazines to the wards. Thus, I was recruited to help deliver the gifts to the patients. We loaded the library carts with gaily wrapped packages. Each door between the wards had to be opened with a key and then carefully locked after each cart was pulled through. Every time I went through, the more alert patients eagerly gathered to see what was happening.

It seems to me, at that time, there were about 3000 adult patients in all the wards. (We were not allowed in the violent patient section of the hospital.) Many of the patients had been institutionalized for years. I will always remember their emotional observations, "This is the first Christmas present I've ever had" with tears running down their faces.

Every year at Christmastime, I reflect on this memorable experience.

One section of Oregon State Hospital was set aside for the counseling and care of alcoholic patients. They had the freedom to go wherever they wanted on the hospital grounds,

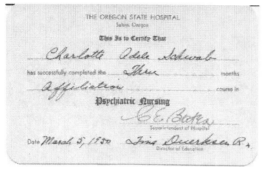

Charlotte carried this with her when she worked at The Oregon State Hospital

so we saw them often. We were told never to fraternize with them. By the way, they were all young and as charming as most alcoholics are. One of the students was smitten and she went on a date with one of her patients. Since she had ignored the order, she was expelled. The next summer I saw her working in a dress shop in Salem. She either ignored me or did not see me. But I naturally figured she had been embarrassed. I never saw her again.

After psychiatry rotation, we moved back to Providence and to our new Nurse's Residence Building. At first, I moved into a single room with bunk beds that had a great view of Mt. Hood and the eastern hills of Portland. Soon, a friend decided to share the room and we both enjoyed the view.

We continued with day classes and floor duty. We rotated either during the afternoon shift or during night duty. Some nights we would be alone with a helper who came in during the very early mornings to help with enemas, blood pressures, and temperatures.

OREGON STATE HOSPITAL
SALEM, OREGON

PSYCHIATRIC NURSING AFFILIATION

Name of Student ____ Miss Charlotte Adele Schmit
School of Nursing ____ Physicians Hospital, Portland, Oregon
Name of Director ____ Ruth E. Beberly, R.N., M.A.
Date of Entering Affiliation ____ December 12, 1949 ____ Total time spent ____ 13 ____ weeks
Total hours of clinical service ____ 270 ____ of special departments ____ 170 ____ hours;
Off duty for illness ____ days; other reasons ____ ; time made up ____ days

Nursing Service or Special Department	Length of Time	Supervisor or Head Nurse
Receiving Service (Men)	3 weeks	Mrs. Francis, R. N.
Medical Surgical Service {Women} {Men}	2 weeks 1 week	Una Kemmerer, R. N. Mrs. Converse, R. N.
Acutely Ill Treatment Service (Women)	3 weeks	Miss Bosdamal, R. N.
Insulin Service		
Bibliotherapy & Occupational Therapy	3 weeks	Mrs. Burke, Therapist
Physiotherapy	1 week	Mrs. Garrett, J. N.

CLASSROOM LECTURES AND GRADES

SUBJECT	HOURS	INSTRUCTOR	GRADE
THEORETICAL	(Total) 60		
Neurology	10	Ruth Jens, R.D.	C
Psychiatry			
(Gen. Principles)	15	Joseph Welch, M.D. }	C
(Functional Psychoses)		L.J. Hiest, M.D.	
(Psychoneuroses)		K.J. Wallace, M.D.	A-
Organic Psychoses		Nursing Instructors	D
Psychiatric Nursing		Lucille M. Higby, R.N.	B-
Mental Hygiene (Elective)			
CLINICAL	(Total) 70	Nursing Instructors as above	
Orientation—Psychiatric Nursing		Special Speakers	
Special Lectures		L.R. Brodie, M.D.	
Clinics		Head Nurses	
Ward Conference		Lucille M. Higby, R.N.	B-
Case Studies		Helen Voorhees, R.N.	C-
Reference Reading			
Physiotherapy		Una Burtbook, R.N. }	B
Recreation, Occupation,		Helen Voorhees, R.N.	
Bibliotherapy			C+
Total Classwork Hours		Class Work (total average)	
Remarks:		Ward Work (total average)	B

Worked well and inspired confidence in her patients by her excellent approach. Average in classroom.

Certificate issued ____ Yes

for ____ three ____ months

Date signed ____ March 6, 1950

Una Duerksen R.N.
Director of Education

E G Bake
Superintendent of Oregon State Hospital

Charlotte's report card for work done in the psych ward at The Oregon State Hospital

The charting was very important, as it gave the doctors and the nursing staff the information about the patient's progress which determined their further treatment. In all this time, it was never boring as we would encounter so many different kinds of people.

One assignment was on the sixth floor, the orthopedic area. This was the ward where all the broken-boned skiers would come to recuperate in their casts. Healing from broken bones takes a long time, so they were kept in bed a very long time. Or did it just seem like a long time? They were very handsome and had to try out their lines on the student nurses. They told stories. They had jokes to share and complained endlessly about having to be taken care of in bed. Always something new was happening on the sixth floor.

This was also the time when a trip to Portland to visit a sick relative took a long time. Family could not come very often from down the valley, so the older patients really appreciated extra attention from a student who could listen to their stories and concerns. As much as we would like to visit with them, we were on a heavy schedule of assignments from the head nurse, our supervisor.

We graduated August 1950.

At graduation ceremonies, we received our pins. Now we had our caps, our capes, and our pins. The next hurdle was the State Board Examinations. The following winter, if we passed all those tests, we would be registered nurses.

After graduation, I went to Salem with plans to take a month off and then begin working at Salem General Hospital. Before the month was over, I was contacted by a family member who needed a nurse to take care of their father because he was recovering from surgery. They already had a nurse during both the day and evening shifts and needed someone to care for him at night. Apprehensive that I had no experience in private-duty nursing, I figured I would just ask the relieving nurse to show me all I needed to know. As soon as he was well and didn't need full-time nursing care, I looked toward securing the job at Salem General.

A few days later, I was contacted again and told that another man, not a family member, desperately needed full-time care. Apparently all the private-duty nurses were already busy and I was their only hope. He was very ill, and he mainly needed to be monitored and given certain medications to keep him comfortable. As a student, I had some experience with the dying process but hadn't been totally responsible, as I was with this gentleman. One morning while I was still at home, I received a phone call that he had died. I mourned as though I was a relative. I felt like I had lost a good friend.

I had already gone through the process to be hired for the night shift at Salem General Hospital. I would be paid $200.00 a month with an extra $10.00 for working the night shift each month. The hospital was directly across from the Oregon State Hospital where I had taken the psychiatry classes. So, the following month I reported to the nurse in charge. She explained all she needed to tell me about the protocol of the floor, and about each patient and the medications and treatments each needed. This was a medical floor. In February, I took the State Board examinations and found out later that I had passed them all except Communicable Diseases. The next exam would be in November. I learned so much from Mrs. Adams the night nurse. (This was the time when the nursing profession was being pressured to unionize. We went to many meetings and she would always play "Devil's Advocate" when any idea was proposed.) I was getting married in July, so I bid my adieu to Salem Hospital and always was thankful for the opportunity they gave me.

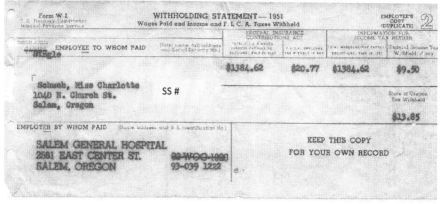

Charlotte's W-2 from Salem General Hospital, 1951.

Charlotte as nurse probie.

SALEM GENERAL HOSPITAL

SALARIES AND PERSONNEL POLICIES FOR NURSES

(Effective July 1, 1950)

DEFINITION:

General Duty Nurse - a graduate, registered nurse employed by a hospital to give expert nursing care to patients.

Assistant Head Nurse - one who is responsible for assisting with administration of nursing service and ward teaching in one unit or division of a unit in a clinical department and for giving expert nursing care.

Head Nurse - one who is responsible for administration of nursing service in one unit or division of a unit in a clinical department and who functions as an assistant supervisor and assistant clinical instructor.

I. SALARIES:

A. Basic Cash salary:
Minimum entrance basic salary, $210.00 (40 hour week).
B. Recognition to be given when a nurse has specialized experience.
C. Salary schedule for other than general duty nurses:
Positions above general staff nursing to be paid commensurate with the position concerned.

II. PERSONNEL POLICIES:

A. Premiums:

1. Assistant Head Nurse, basic salary plus $10.00 per month.
2. Evening and night duty, basic salary plus $10.00 per month.
3. If on call for O.B. and Surgery, basic salary plus $10.00 extra per month and time off for actual overtime on duty to be made up in 30 days.

B. Tenure of Service:

At the end of the first six months of service, an increase of $5.00 per month; at the end of twelve months, increase of $5.00; at the end of 24 months, an increase of $5.00; at the end of 36 months, an increase of $5.00. Nurses who have been employed in a hospital for a number of years when this policy goes into effect shall be entitled to the salary increments herein established for their length of service.

C. Maintenance:

Meal tickets may be purchased at the office. Breakfast $.25; Lunch, $.25; Dinner, $.50; Supper, $.25.

D. Room:

Temporary quarters in Nurses' Home at $25.00 per month may be used until suitable quarters are secured elsewhere.

Salaries and policies for the nurses at Salem General Hospital, 1950. Page 1

E. Laundry:

No laundry facilities at Hospital. Commercial laundry services available.

F. Vacations:

A minimum of two weeks vacation shall be granted out of each twelve months continuous service. No vacation will be granted until the individual has been employed a minimum of six months, when one calendar week may be allowed.

Terminal vacations to be granted after twelve months continuous service, provided 14 days notice of intended resignation has been submitted.

G. Sick Leave:

Sick leave with pay is granted by the hospital on the following conditions:

1. One day sick leave per month with pay will be allowed for each month of employment, cumulative to sixty calendar days.

2. Pay for sick leave is to begin with the second day of each illness.

3. Unused sick leave is not to be interpreted as time accumulated toward vacation. This accumulated sick leave is for the protection and security of the nurse in cases of extended illness.

H. Hospital Insurance and Rest Periods:

1. Hospital insurance is strongly recommended for all nurses. Pay roll deduction plan is to be made available by the Hospital.

2. One 10 minute rest period is to be allowed during each 8 hour period of employment.

I. Hours of Work:

1. The basic work week shall be 40 hours.

2. The basic work day shall be eight (8) consecutive hours, exclusive of the lunch period, which shall be on the nurses own time.

3. Overtime to be made up by time off according to the hospitals policy. Overtime shall accrue only if 30 minutes or more of overtime have been worked. Any allowable overtime must be properly authorized.

4. The following six (6) holidays shall be granted with regular pay: New Years Day, Memorial Day, Fourth of July, Labor Day, Thanksgiving and Christmas Day.

5. It is agreed that holiday work shall be rotated by the hospital and that those nurses required to work shall have a compensatory day off with regular pay within thirty (30) days, or 1 additional days pay in lieu of compensatory day off.

6. If a holiday occurs on a nurses regular day off, she is to receive a compensatory day off with pay within thirty (30) days. If a holiday falls during the nurse's vacation, an extra day of vacation is to be given or an extra day of pay is to be added to her vacation pay.

Salaries and policies for the nurses at Salem General Hospital, 1950. Page 2

7. Weekly time schedule and days off to be posted five (5) days prior to the commencement of that week.

J. Staff Relief:

General duty nursing, where the hospital offers less that 14 consecutive working days is to be considered staff relief. The daily fee for staff relief should be the same as the prevailing fee for 8 hour private duty. When a nurse prefers to work only 1 or 2 days a week, she is to be paid the general duty monthly salary prorated for the applicable number of days worked.

K. Termination of Employment:

1. Nurses are to give not less than 14 days notice of intended resignation.

2. Hospitals are to give 14 days notice of dismissal or 14 days pay in lieu of notice, except that no notice need be given if nurses are discharged for cause.

L. Professional Development:

1. After one year of continuous employment, permission may be granted for leave of absence without pay for study, not to exceed one calendar year, without loss of accrued benefits.

2. Leave of absence without pay may be granted to attend professional meetings provided the number of nurses wishing to attend such meetings will not jeopardize the hospital service.

3. An absence of more than 90 days terminates all privileges, tenure and sick leave unless properly authorized.

4. All hospitals are urged to check the current Oregon State registration of all nurses promptly at the time of employment and thereafter upon request.

M. Social Security as soon as available.

N. Rotation:

1. Unless a nurse chooses to work 3-11 or 11-7 these shifts should be rotated.

2. Rotation plans should be worked out and posted two weeks in advance of effective date.

3. Nurses who decline rotation and/or assignment when necessary shall be paid at the rate of 10% below the applicable base rate of pay. Such nurses will be entitled to salary increments as they accrue.

O. Health:

1. The hospital shall arrange to take chest x-rays of nurses within one week after employment, and annually thereafter, at no cost to the nurse.

2. Nurses shall be permitted serological examination at no expense to themselves when indicated because of exposure to contagious disease.

Salaries and policies for the nurses at Salem General Hospital, 1950. Page 3

Dear Charlotte,

Well, what a surprise! It seems girls never learn – They do it every time. Well, if this Norman Schmidt is as good as you are you should both be happy. Sorry this will not reach you before the Big Day. Received the notice only _just now_ my little wedding gift shall be that I offer Holy Mass for you on July 14th. God bless you – shall surely see you when I return to US. Love to _all_ of you

Father Alcuin OSB

Capital Journal Newspaper
Wednesday, July 18, 1951
Salem Oregon

The wedding of Miss Charlotte Schwab, daughter of Mrs. Paul Schwab of Salem, and Norman Schmidt of Lebanon, was an event of Saturday morning, July 14, in St. Vincent's Catholic Church. Father Reedy, pastor, performed the 10 o'clock ceremony.

Music was provided by Miss Helen Keber of Mt. Angel, who played the organ and Miss Pauline Saalfeld and Miss Eustelle Bauman, both of Mt. Angel, who sang.

The bride, given in marriage by her grandfather, Frank Fisher, wore a white satin gown fashioned with a fitted bodice with Queen Ann lace collar, buttons down the front, long sleeves, and a long train. A fingertip length veil was arranged from a lace crown. The bride carried a white orchid on a prayer book from which cascaded streamers tied with stephanotis.

Maid of honor was Miss Marlene Schwab, sister of the bride, who wore an orchid gown made with lace bodice and taffeta skirt. She wore a yellow carnation headdress and carried a nosegay of yellow carnations with yellow ribbon.

Bridesmaids, Mrs. Dale Stewart of Lebanon and Mrs. Robert Gillas of Vancouver, Wash., wore gowns like the hoor attendant's and carried nosegays of lavender sweet peas with green ribbons. They wore headbands of orchid sweet peas.

Best man for his brother was Lawrence Schmidt and groomsmen were Dale Stewart of Lebanon and Vernon Tracy of Salem. Ushers were Peter Schmidt, brother of the bridegroom, and Leo Schwab, uncle of the bride.

The bride's mother wore a navy blue outfit with white accessories and a corsage of Cecile Brunner roses.

A wedding breakfast was served at the Camellia room of the Senator hotel following the ceremony. Those attending were the bridal party and relatives of the couple.

The Izaak Walton hall was the scene of the reception in the afternoon. Miss Verda Powell and Miss Ann Wilkins, both of Portland, cut the cake. Mrs. Leonard Fisher and Mrs. Leo Schwab, aunts of the bride, served punch and Miss Kathryn Schmidt, sister of the bridegroom, poured coffee. Miss Beverly Lebold and Miss Virginia Lovcik were in charge of the gift table and Miss Isabelle Schmidt, sister of the bridegroom, passed the guest book. Assisting about the rooms were Miss Ruth Wilde, Miss Joan Fisher and Miss Marie Schmidt, cousins of the couple.

Following a wedding trip to California, the couple will make their home at 203 Loma Alta. Los Gatos, Calif. For going away the bride chose a beige silk faille dress with brown accessories and the orchid from her bridal bouquet.

Norm and Charlotte's wedding announcement

Norm and Charlotte's wedding.

(Sunshine)

July 14, 1957 - left Salem - the Rim "beautiful"
@ 4:20 p.m. drove to Leb-
hello to Dale; to Sweet Home,
goodbye to Leo; to Clear
Lake "no cabins"; to
Suttle Lake stayed over
July 15, 1957. Long distance
nite & up @ 6:00 a.m. on
way to eat - Had to
clean off all writing on
car first.
Drove to Bend - ate
breakfast - went to Mass
at 8:00 a.m. Drove to
Crater Lake & around

Notes from Charlotte and Norm's honeymoon trip.

part two

The Busy Years

Wedding Reception and Trip South

Salem – July 14, 1951

We put our wedding gifts in the trunk and in the back seat of our car. Along with all the other gifts was the Lane Cedar Chest, a wedding gift from Norm. After saying our thank yous and goodbyes we left Salem at 4:20pm. Norm's groomsmen had decorated the car with white shoe polish and rocks in the hubcaps. It was a noisy exit.

We drove to Lebanon, washed off the car, and took out the rocks and continued east through Sweet Home and the forested mountains along highway 20. We stopped at Clear Lake and were told that their cabins were all occupied. Our next choice was beautiful Suttle Lake. The attendant told us that they had one cabin left and it was at the bottom of the hill. We decided to take it because it was a perfect spot for our first night as husband and wife.

Our lovely quiet was disturbed, though, whenever anyone used the water in the other cabins. Since we were at the bottom of the hill, we were serenaded by the gurgling water pipes as the water rushed downhill. Early the next morning, we drove to Bend and went to Mass. We had breakfast and then drove to Crater Lake and drove around the Rim.

"There could not be anything more beautiful in God's world," I wrote in my wedding journal. The sky was blue, and the weather looked warm as we enjoyed our lunch in the Lodge overlooking the blue waters of Crater Lake.

After lunch, we drove to the House of Mystery at the Oregon Vortex in Gold Hill, Oregon and enjoyed being tourists at this natural phenomenon. We were on our way to stay the night in Grants Pass, Oregon.

The next morning, we drove to The Oregon Caves and went on a guided tour. The guide took us underground and showed us inside the mountain. They had a wooden stairway going down. The guide turned off the lights and everything got dark. Norm kissed me in this romantic setting and the sound of the kiss echoed throughout the cave. Everyone in our group laughed as the lights were turned back on.

We drove curving highway 199 through a heavily forested area on our way to Crescent City, California. Highway 101 was also a curving two-lane road along the Pacific Ocean and through the Redwood Forest. We were excited by the amazing sight of the gigantic redwoods as they towered over us.

We continued south to San Rafael, California to visit with Sr. Bernice, Norm's older sister who had joined the Benedictine Sisters when she was 13 years old. She was there attending classes at the Dominican College in San Rafael, California. As she was unable to come to the wedding, we brought the top layer of our wedding cake to celebrate with her. We stopped at a store to get some vanilla ice cream to go with the cake and then drove to the college as planned. We visited with Sr. Bernice and Sr. Carol, had cake and ice cream, and filled them with the stories of our wedding and our travels. It was a beautiful, sunny afternoon. Since they both had classes to attend, we bid our farewells.

Our next stop was our new home in Los Gatos, California.

How We Decided
on California

Norm had completed his high school education in three years so he could join the Army [during World War II]. His brother, Leo, was serving in the Third Army in the European front with General Patton. His brother, Larry, joined the Army Air Corps and flew P38's in Europe [photo reconnaissance].

Norm was assigned to basic training in Fort Bragg, North Carolina, then he was sent to Japan with the Army of Occupation for eight months [at the end of the war] then came home on furlough for three weeks. His next assignment was to Fort Ord, California.

As he had a 1941 Oldsmobile car and could leave the base after his assignment was completed, he could drive all around the area enjoying the Seventeen Mile Drive along the Pacific coast. He especially enjoyed watching the construction of the Pebble Beach Golf Course [regarded as the most beautiful course in the world] and the other buildings around the course overlooking the rugged shoreline of the Pacific Ocean.

As we were talking about our future plans, he told me how much he enjoyed that trip to California and shared with me its beauty. Norm had been working jobs out of the Electrical Union shop in Salem and they were becoming harder to find, so he had worked at the Standard Gas Station in downtown Lebanon for eight months. He had wanted to get back to his profession as an electrician.

He spoke to the Union representative in Salem and found that there were jobs in construction out of the San Jose, California Union Shop. We talked about the idea of a trip to San Jose to see what we thought of it. We talked to Isabelle, his sister he was living with before we got married, about coming along with us to see how things looked. She came along and enjoyed the trip as much as we did. Norm was so anxious to get there he drove until he was tired. That night we slept in the car and continued at daybreak.

When we arrived, he drove to the Union Hall and asked about work there as an electrician. They could assign him wherever he was needed. A big shopping center was being built in Santa Clara and workers in all areas would be needed.

So now we needed a place to live.

A home in Los Gatos (a quiet little town on the road to the coast and Santa Cruz) looked appealing. The owner was renting her basement apartment. Norm paid the first month's rent to hold it until we returned after our wedding. After driving to Santa Cruz and down the coast, we were excited to start planning our return.

As it was spring, the days were sunny and the possibilities of living in that beautiful place with all the colorful flowers was exhilarating. We couldn't wait to get back.

Los Gatos, California

After settling in Los Gatos, we explored the many attractions along the roads out of town. We found Santa Claus, California near Carpentaria in a small area along the road to the coast. We remarked that it was Christmas year-round in that sunny area of California.

Santa Cruz, CA also captivated us with its boardwalk with carnival rides and many booths with prize winning games. There were many large homes with an expansive view of the town and a breathtaking view of the Pacific Ocean.

But we were happy in our new basement apartment home in Los Gatos. As a small town with easy access to stores for shopping, it was easy for me to get around without a car. Norm took the car to work, so I had the days to explore the small businesses and found the owners pleasant and helpful. Mr. and Mrs. Malatesta were a charming older couple who had been in the appliance business for many years. They welcomed a chat with a newcomer to their town. They suggested interesting places for us to see on the weekends and gave us a few tips about interesting things that were happening in town.

During weekends, we drove many hilly curved roads around the area. I remember Mountain View, Sunnyvale, and Cupertino. The electrical union office was in San Jose. Norm's first job was a shopping center being built in Santa Clara. On Sundays we attended Mass at the cathedral in San Jose. (We also visited Marie Rice who still lives in San Jose. Marie and husband Jim were friends of Larry Schmidt. The men were in the service together.) We also drove to San Francisco and crossed huge bridges on our sightseeing explorations. Our drives took us many places in that beautiful scenery. I was as enchanted with the Seventeen Mile drive on the curving roads overlooking the Pacific Ocean as Norm had been when he was in training at Fort Ord.

One Saturday evening we drove to the Clairmont Hotel as they were presenting "A musical evening with the Ray Anthony Big Band." We had enough money for the cover charge and a few drinks. An older couple had a table nearby. Very likely they could tell we were newlyweds and purchased a drink for us. We waved our thanks across the ballroom.

After thoroughly enjoying our evening of dancing to the mellow music, we floated out the front door of the hotel and walked down the hill to where our car was parked.

Those were the carefree days.....................

Our friends who had introduced us, Dale and Shirley Stewart, came to visit soon after we arrived. Our landlady, Frieda, had said the basement apartment rule was: No Smoking

Allowed. As they came to the doorway, Dale had a lit cigarette in his hand, so he put it out in the dirt of the flower bed next to the front door of the apartment. He also had a box of bottles of beer under his arm.

As I was making dinner in our new pressure cooker, I put some meat, potatoes and carrots in. When the timer (according to the directions) indicated the meal was ready, I made the grand announcement that dinner was served. I must not have followed all the directions because the food started exploding out of the top almost hitting the ceiling. After we cleaned up the mess (and remarked about my lack of cooking skills), there was enough food left in the pot so we could have dinner. We couldn't help laughing about it.

For many years when we visited with them, the topic came up again about Charlotte's first cooking attempt. And the laughter followed................

After that day, we found a letter at our door. It was from our landlady, Freida.

203 Loma Alta Ave.,
Los Gatos, Calif.
July 28, 1951.

TO:

Mr. & Mrs. Norman Schmidt,
203 Loma Alta Avenue,
Los Gatos, Calif.

I regret that I have to notify you to
move from the apartment.

My sister is going to occupy her own
home by September 1st, however should you find
another lodging before that time it would be
appreciated very much.

Yours very truly,

Frieda Wihler

(Frieda Wihler)

Letter from Frieda asking Norm and Charlotte to move out.

Move to San Jose

When we received Frieda's letter, we knew we had done something unforgivable. Our next pursuit was to find another place to live. We drove all around and found some tract homes that had recently been built in an old area of a prune orchard in San Jose. The only way we could afford to buy was to sell the 1950 Chevrolet; so we did.

The houses all had one bedroom with a living room, kitchen, bathroom and a carport, that were being built to accommodate first-time house buyers in the area. Many had been sold before we got there. This particular one was very livable but had fly specks on the walls in every room.

It would take us a long time to wash down all the walls, so another couple we had met said they would come and help us. They were the answer to our prayers.

Now to furnish the place..............We purchased a second-hand couch, gas cooking stove, and bed set. We already had our kitchen supplies, so we were ready to move in. As now we did not have a car, Norm's boss, Ted De Nio picked Norm up each morning and took him to work. They were working on the job at the shopping center.

One Saturday, Ted came by and told Norm jokingly that he was tired of hauling him to work and they were going to get him a car. Norm's reply was, "I haven't got a down payment on a postage stamp." Their next stop was a used car lot. The owner showed them what he had. Norm picked out a 1937 Pontiac and the owner said he thought it didn't take oil and that it was in good condition. The down payment was $75. Norm had $20 and Ted loaned him $55. We paid $17 each month until we traded it in years down the road. It had turned out to be in very good condition.

Receipt for Packard Bell TV

Norm worked at the shopping center for six months. We drove by the job location one day and he showed me what he and the other electricians had been installing. Very soon after that, we saw shopping centers being built wherever we went. The area was growing.

Our next purchase was a TV set from the Malatesta Appliance Store. TV's had been perfected so there was clear reception everywhere in the San Jose area. The early shows were mostly children's shows and local productions of national shows. We enjoyed "Show of Shows" with Sid Caesar, Imogean Coca and other comedians of the era. The broadcasts started at 6 AM and ended at midnight.

Our first guest was Isabelle. She took the train from Albany to San

Isabel Schmidt

Jose for the Christmas holidays. The couch in the living room became her bed and she said she was very comfortable there. As that was the location of the TV set, she became an excited fan of everything that was on and watched until the set went

Paul and Isabel Osterman

off the air each night at midnight. While Isabelle was our visitor, we celebrated Christmas dinner at Marie Rice's home in San Jose. We also met Marie and Jim's daughter and her family. It was a joyful reunion with Marie's family.

Isabelle spent a week with us and then took the train back to her home in Oregon.

Top right: Norm's brother Larry Schmidt and his wife Shirley Cone-Schmidt

Bottom: Charlotte's sister Lois's wedding to Vern Tracy. Pictured is Bud Laughley on the left, Marlene in front, Dotie Ault behind Marlene, Lois and Vernon walking out of the church after they got married. Man in front with what looks like a mohawk, Roland Eastlant. Charlotte is looking back at Ruth and Leonard Orton

Moving back to Oregon

The construction of the shopping center was almost completed. The electricians had been working for six months and now their job would be done. Norm's boss, Ted De Nio, contacted the Union shop and was given permission to assign Norm to work out of Hansen's Electric in Campbell, California. Norm's next job was wiring new houses that were being built in the area.

As January ended, the rains came and the jobs were shut down. We had many discussions about going back to Oregon.

Norm said that it would be better to raise the children where there were relatives and friends close by. Being pregnant with our first child gave us a new perspective on our lives and what the future might be for them. We made plans to leave the house and car and purchased two tickets on the train to take us to the Albany, Oregon railroad station.

Ted and his wife Bonnie drove us and our luggage to board the train at the station in San Jose. Norm had notified

Isabelle that we were coming and the time that we would arrive. He also called Dale to see if he could pick us up at the Albany train depot.

Norm's friend from Lebanon, Jim Haskell, owned two upstairs furnished apartments in Lebanon. Our friends Dale and Shirley were renting one and we rented the other one.

After Norm had me settled, he took the bus back to San Jose, sold the house, rented a trailer and put our furniture in it, hooked the car to the trailer and headed to Lebanon.

When he got back with our furniture we settled into a ground floor apartment in downtown Lebanon. We had been there a few weeks when Isabelle offered to let us move into her home in Lebanon until the baby was born and Norm could find a permanent job.

Charlotte with Ric and Lois's daughter Gayle

On May 22, 1952, our baby was born at Lebanon General Hospital. Dr. Irvine delivered Ric [Norman Eric Jr.] and we were blessed to have such an experienced professional who recognized that the umbilical cord was around the baby's neck and could successfully remove it as the baby was born.

Ric was a good baby. The summer of 1952 was very hot in Lebanon. We pulled down all the shades on the windows in the house to keep out as much heat as possible. I vividly remember him wearing only diapers and playing on his blanket on the

Ric with Norm, 1952/53

floor of the living room. Norm purchased an oscillating fan from Jim at the store which helped move the air around.

Ric was baptized in Lebanon, Oregon at St. Edward's Church with many relatives and friends in attendance. During this time, we stayed in Isabelle's home until Norm was hired in Salem as an electrician at Oregon Pulp and Paper Company in the autumn of 1952.

So it looked like I would be moving back to Salem!

Top: Ric in high chair

Middle picture: LuAnn and Ric

Bottom: Ric with his Christmas train set.

Moving to Salem

We rented an upstairs apartment at 5055 N. Lancaster Drive, Salem, and lived there until February 28, 1953 when we purchased a house at 4025 Earl Ave. The house was in a small neighborhood on a short street, east of downtown Salem.

My sister Marlene had finished beauty school in Portland

Ric on the right, with LuAnn in the middle and Craig Hoy to the left. On or around 1954

and was working at a salon in Salem and living in an apartment close to the salon. Then she decided to marry John Hoy. Their wedding Mass was in a chapel in the woods at Crooked Finger which is a spot close to Scotts Mills, Oregon. A close family friend, Father Hildebrand, officiated at their wedding Mass that was attended by families and friends. It was a beautiful day in beautiful surroundings.

During the time we lived in Salem, my mother Eleanor married her second husband, Tiny Frey. Mother and my

Marlene and her niece.

brother, Ron, moved to Tiny's home in Mt. Angel, Oregon. Since both of my sisters and their families lived in Salem, too, we all had many opportunities to see Mother and Ron in Mt. Angel. Mother and Tiny took many trips to the ocean and the desert where they were married and visited their priest friend that had a parish in southeastern Oregon. She continued to play Bridge and Pinochle with her friends.

One morning I drove to Mt. Angel to see Mother. As I was driving east on Silverton Road, following the curve, I saw a car sideways on the road coming toward my car. I pulled off the road as far as I could because a big ditch was next to the side of the road. And I stopped.

These were the days of no seatbelts or car seats for children. Two-year-old Ric had been seated as we drove, but as I stopped, he stood on the front seat beside me. At that moment, the car hit and he flew into the windshield.

LuAnn

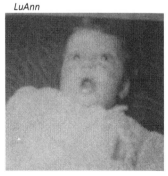

Six-week-old LuAnn [born May 20, 1954] was sleeping on the backseat wrapped in blankets, the safest place for babies at that time. The impact threw her little body to the floor and she began to scream. I tried to get out of the car and my door wouldn't open. I grabbed Ric and held him and tried to find

Ric and LuAnn

something to put on his bleeding head.

People from the houses next to the highway were there before I knew it. A nice lady opened the back door and took the screaming baby out of the back seat saying she was taking her to a house that she pointed out to me. It seemed the ambulance came immediately. The men got the door open, so I got out and ran to the house where the kind ladies had taken the children.

The paramedic did what he could for Ric's bloody head, checked the baby and took us all to the hospital. The doctors checked us all over, x-rayed my knees and said we did not have any broken bones. The Doctor told me that when I grew old I would

LuAnn and Ric

have arthritis in my knees. I remember laughing and saying, "I'll never grow old."

Jim Haskell loaned Norm his car so he could go to where the wreck occurred. We had already been taken to the hospital, so he found us there. We never did find out anything about the driver and why her car was sliding down the highway.

Jim came each day to take Norm to work until Norm could find another car for us to buy.

Norm, Ric, and LuAnn

Memories of Mother

Mother had been diagnosed with breast cancer in 1952. Her doctor operated on her and found that the biopsy indicated the cancer cells had metastasized. I remember standing at the window of the nurse's station and looking onto a rainy morning. The feelings I had are hard to describe: sadness, loss, an empty feeling in my heart, and the tears flowed. There were not many treatments in those years. She was under the care of the doctors in a clinic in Salem. I remember how she suffered after the radiation burned her skin. That was only one of the many treatment appointments that I drove her to in Salem and then back to her home in Mt. Angel to rest. In all that time I do not remember her complaining and she had every reason to be upset or questioning.

Mother told me that she felt that the breast cancer was caused by the stress of the death of her husband. (Many years later, a friend of mine asked me to attend a program with her.

A psychiatrist friend of hers was speaking at the local college. His program was well-attended and after his speech was over he asked for questions. It was an opportunity for me to see what he thought about Mother's belief. He was very sincere when he told me that the kind of stress that a death of a spouse can bring, can indeed cause disease.)

One day, Mother told me that she had an appointment with a lawyer to set up her will. She asked me to go with her. We had already discussed Ron and that he would come to live with us and our family. As the process of my being Ron's guardian needed to be legal, I had to sign some papers.

When she became bedridden, we would visit even more often. I remember asking if any of her friends had been by to visit. These were women that she played cards with and worked on church and school related projects with. She then told me that not many of them had come by. At this time, not much was known about breast cancer and her friends were concerned that it might be contagious. I knew better than that because of my training. (It is hard to believe, but that's a fear that I still hear in present-day conversations.)

One day, a young priest came by to visit and Mother told him that she did not feel that she could pray for herself anymore. He told her all the prayers she had said, and that others had said for her, were helping her now through these difficult days.

One weekend, Norm and I went to visit Mother. As we entered her room she took off the patch that she had been wearing to cover her left eye and laughingly said, "Hi Norm, I'm in a hell of a shape." [Charlotte's memory is that the patch was there, but she doesn't recall why. We called Ron to see if he remembered, and he said that it had something to do with the cancer, but he didn't know what.]

We had spent the day with Mother and were there the evening when she died. As Tiny's house was big with a big backyard, the children (Marlene's, Lois's, and mine) played together outside while we were with Mother inside. It was turning dark, so Lois decided to take the children home and put them to bed. We could hear Mother's labored breathing. Her soul waited to leave her until she was all alone in her room. She died on October 9, 1954.

She and Tiny had earlier decided that they each would be buried next to their spouses of their first marriages. Mother was buried next to Daddy in Mt. Angel Cemetery. The location is next to the roadway entrance on the right side of the entrance.

The priests who gave the homilies at her funeral Mass were old friends who had been to our home frequently when

Eleanor's Funeral Card

we were young. Each one marveled at how dedicated Mother was as a widow raising four children.

After the funeral and reception were over, we brought Ron back to Salem to live with us. Ron was fifteen years old and attended his junior year of school at Sacred Heart Academy in downtown Salem. As the Catholic school children could not ride the school buses, Ron and a neighborhood classmate drove to school together in his classmate's car.

In April, he celebrated his sixteenth birthday and became fascinated with antique cars. He purchased a 1929 Ford Model A. Ron has many memories of his first experience owning a car.

Ric was growing fast. Norm was adding onto the house in his spare time with Ric wanting to help him. That Christmas, Santa brought him some little tools and he wore his tool belt proudly.

Norm decided to purchase an American Flyer train set. He said that Ric was old enough to enjoy playing with trains. Norm and Ron put the rails together and they had fun watching the train go over the tracks. Ric decided he wanted to play with them and as he crawled next to them they both brushed him away. I asked why they didn't include him in the play and Norm said he would be included when the train was all set up. Somehow that time did not come for several months.

Norm with LuAnn and Ric

We lived in the Earl Ave. house for two and one-half years. Norm had been at the paper mill in Salem working different shifts and meeting the men that had been there many years. He felt he had done a good job for the company.

Charlotte with Ric and LuAnn

A new paper mill was being built south of Salem in Albany, Oregon on Highway 5. One of the men Norm worked with was hired there and rumors were that it was to be a big project. Norm received a phone call from the Electrical Department representative offering him a Chief Electrician position. He would be hired to build the electrical department. Without hesitation, Norm accepted the job. We rented the house to a family and prepared our move.

Ric on the Plymouth

Moving to Albany, Oregon
1955-1960/61

Norm found a grand old house in downtown Albany for us to rent. In Salem, I had my regular OB/GYN doctor who had been recommended to me while I was expecting LuAnn. I continued regular visits and LuAnn had her checkups and vaccinations.

After 8 months I had the familiar symptoms of pregnancy again. I continued my visits to the doctor and he said the new baby would be born in October. So, before our move to Albany, I saw the doctor again and told him that we would be moving but I would be coming back for my checkups.

Norm was scheduled to report for his new job at Western Kraft on Sept. 6, 1955. We settled into the big house, 3 bedrooms upstairs and living room, kitchen etc. on the main floor and in the basement was the oil heating system. Norm reported to the mill, spending long hours at his job.

September in Oregon can be very beautiful. We were comfortable in the big home. Some mornings Ric, LuAnn, and I would take a walk around town. Ric had a tricycle and I pulled LuAnn in the red wagon. Everything was new to us so we explored a park and saw a furniture store, a fire station, a bakery, a big hotel and the Linn County Courthouse. We also found a place for ice cream treats called Hasty Freeze.

One night, the baby indicated that he was ready to show up. We took a hurried car ride to the hospital in Salem. The doctor was waiting for us and my labor was short, resulting in a beautiful healthy baby boy.

Frank Martin was born September 15, 1955. His first name came from my Grandfather Frank Fisher who was a happy and kind man. Martin was the name of our parish priest, Father Doherty, who was also a kind and happy man. He loved to travel in the winter to warm destinations with his sisters from Chicago.

Frank, Ric, and LuAnn, Christmas, 1956

After the obligatory 3 days in the hospital, we took the baby home to Albany. I remembered that I had been wondering how I could take care of another child as the days were already filled. Somehow Frank was so easy to take care of that he just fit into our schedule.

Looking back, that was a lesson I learned. If you really love something or someone the time will open up. Life sure teaches beautiful lessons but I guess we have to experience them first.

Frank and Ric at Christmas, 1956

We settled again into our downtown Albany house and started our new routine.

All went well until the cold, windy weather came. The house had been built many years before and the cold air came in through the windows and under the doors. I put towels under the doors and newspaper in the cracks of the window sills.

One day the heat would not come on, so I called Norm at work. When he came and discovered that the oil barrel was empty, he figured out we had gone through 150 gallons of oil in less than a month.

The warm air must have been heating the outside instead of the inside.

LuAnn and Frank

Top: Frank, LuAnn, and Ric
Middle left: Frank and LuAnn
Middle right: Frank, LuAnn, and Ric
Bottom: Ric, LuAnn, and Frank

2720 South Geary Street

Norm decided we would need to find a more economical place to live. In his spare time, he found a new ranch style house on Geary Street, two miles from downtown Albany. It would be just right for all of us.

Ron would have the front bedroom, Ric and Frank would share a room and LuAnn would have a bedroom. Norm and I would have the back bedroom and the bathroom. There was a bigger bathroom off the hallway. The living room had a fireplace and the dining room was at the end of the living room. Around the corner was the kitchen with a large window view of the backyard and fields of grain. Tucked into a closet with a folding door was the perfect place for the washer and dryer. The floors were a beautiful hardwood.

There was a carport with a furnace room in front of the house and a big grassy area in the front and side yards. We had gotten a settlement from the insurance company for the accident on Silverton Road and we used that money for a down payment on the house.

As we were on a tight budget, we moved in with what household items we had and carefully purchased towel hangers and other miscellaneous items that a new house requires.

For many years, we kept a tight budget and recorded everything we purchased in our budget ledger. We had been so careful with handling Norm's paycheck that I was surprised when he told me one day not to send the Sears delivery man away as he was bringing a chest freezer and would put it in the furnace room. BECAUSE I WOULD HAVE DONE THAT!!!! After Norm explained that now we could buy items in bulk and store them for later use, I started shopping with future meals in mind.

Himalayan blackberry bushes grow wild in Oregon and often when the little ones were napping I would walk across the street and pick the ripe berries for the evening cobbler and then put some into the freezer.

We also purchased beef from an electrician who worked with Norm. He had a farm where he and his family lived.

When we moved to Albany, Ron found a job as a box boy at Erickson's grocery store. He worked after school and during the winter holidays. He sold his model A antique car in Salem and purchased a Pontiac which was also more dependable. Ron met Bob Hunt shortly after school started and they became lifelong friends. Bob's dad Roy was a retired state police officer who treated Ron as a close relative. Ron probably spent more time at Mr. and Mrs. Hunt's house than with us. Ron needed a father figure and Roy Hunt certainly filled that need. The number of times Ron quoted Roy's words to the boys in their conversations, helped me understand his kind way.

Medical Miracle

The baby boy was born October 10, 1956 without a name. We talked about names and decided that no one else we know had the name Jacob and it went perfectly with Schmidt. Now we needed a middle name that is strong too and decided on John. So, the baby was to be named Jacob John Schmidt; a good strong name.

In my training to become a nurse, classes were taught to the new mothers on how to breast feed their newborns and how to take care of them. The

Norm with Ric, Baby Jake, and LuAnn

instructors stressed the baby's immunity boost with Mother's milk and other details. So, because of that, and my experience with our other children, I could see that there was something wrong when I nursed Jacob the first time. He spit up a big mouthful of brownish liquid. I notified the OB nurse and she let the doctor know that something wasn't working right.

I contacted a nurse friend and told her about Jacob and asked her to call Fr. Doherty, so he could come and baptize Jacob, worried that there was something seriously wrong. Father came and baptized Jacob John and blessed the Doctor's decisions and Jacob's care.

Frank and Jake

Plans were then made to take the baby to Good Samaritan Hospital in Portland, some 75 miles north of Albany. A specialist, Dr. McKredie, was flying up from San Francisco and would do the surgery as soon as he arrived. Norm and a friend bundled the baby up and they drove to Portland.

When Norm came back to my hospital room, many hours later, he said tiny Jacob had survived the removal of a section of his intestines that had been twisted. The area removed had been gangrenous and if it hadn't been removed, Jacob would have died.

Ten days later after checking on him every day, Norm and a friend drove to get him from the hospital. It was a good thing that Jacob's birth weight was about 10 lbs. because when he came back from Good Samaritan he looked like a prisoner of war, just skin and bones.

Norm came back with very specific instructions: feed him 4 oz. of formula every 4 hours then put him in the crib to sleep and give him a chance to heal. The most important change we should next expect would be a bowel movement to prove that the baby's intestines were healed and working. We were overjoyed when that naturally happened, and the baby gained weight and recovered over many months.

Our local pediatrician took very good care of Jacob. As little as he was, 1.5 days old when the doctors operated, each time when he saw either the doctor or the nurse's white jacket he screamed. Eventually, Jacob and the pediatrician became good friends and even in middle school he wanted to have his school physicals from him.

As a baby, Jacob did not want to be held and as a spunky little guy he learned to walk early on. He is curious about everything and at 51 he is good-looking, friendly, and knows no strangers. His energy level slows down only when he sleeps.

One day I started remembering again all that had happened with baby Jacob. In those days we didn't have as much research as we have these days. Because of that, many babies didn't survive. When babies were born, and they had issues like Jacob had, parents were only allowed an hour each day to visit their child in Pediatrics. An hour each day. Oh, how we have changed!

Now, research and common sense, have proven how very important touch and caressing is to the skin of a newborn.

The doctors' stern rules to put the baby down in the crib so he could heal was very hard for me as I wanted to hold him as I had held many children since before I was nine.

Back: Ric and LuAnn
Front: Jake and Frank

Ellen Marie

One vivid memory: we were all gathered in Chuck and Doris Coffey's backyard when Chuck was convinced that he saw a "flying saucer." We all watched his sighting and after a time it flew over the horizon. We talked about that for years — was it or wasn't it? Many things in life don't have any answers but are still fun to remember.

The six years that we lived in our ranch home were busy with school, parent teacher meetings, trips to the grocery store, birthday parties, Labor Day picnics, Western Kraft Christmas parties at the hotel in Salem, visits with family in Lebanon, and so many other happy gatherings.

The mill was expanding again. The #2 machine was built to make a lighter paper which was used for grocery bags. Norm worked long hours.

During the summer, we took vacations at the beach. During the winter, we played in the snow in the mountains close by.

We were totally blessed. The children were growing and healthy. Norm was enjoying his job and learning about new equipment that needed to be ordered every day.

One day, LuAnn and I were at the kitchen table folding warm clothes from the dryer and she said, "We need more girls around here."

I said, "I guess we had better pray for some girls for our family."

Little did I know at that time that I was pregnant. So, LuAnn received her gift of a baby girl. Ellen Marie was born January 9, 1958.

She had a hard time deciding when she wanted to be born. The signs of labor were there, but she was taking a little longer. We went to the hospital, I was checked over and the nurse said that the baby would be born when she was ready and recommended I walk the halls. I had heard of that method of encouraging the contractions and it worked. She did come when she was ready!!

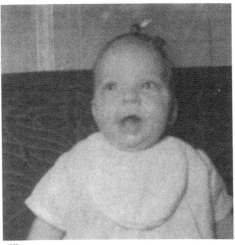

Ellen

For some reason I had to stay in the hospital for 5 days. Apparently, the doctor noticed something and wanted to monitor me. Maybe I just needed a good rest!!

Anyhow, it gave Ellen and me some extra time together before we joined the family who were eagerly awaiting her arrival at home. The one most excited was LuAnn.

We developed a new routine of family life and little Ellen enjoyed all the attention. Before lunch each day, the children would play in the front yard and I would sit in a chair watching their activities and mending the holey socks that I had collected from the dryer.

Frank, a cousin, Jake, and little Ellen

The busy road in front of our house had ditches on both sides. I worried that one of the children would wander off because our yard where they played wasn't fenced off. We purchased a swing set and Norm set it up beside the house, further away from the road, to encourage the children to play farther away from the street. Now they had the wagon, a small bicycle, the tricycle, and the swing set. Sometimes the neighborhood pre-school children found their way over to play in our yard, too.

When lunch and naptime came, all the visiting children went to their own homes.

We lived just twelve miles from Lebanon, where Norm's relatives lived. We visited them, and they came over to see us when they could. We also spent many holidays together.

The Schmidt family reunion was held at one of the homes each summer when Sister Bernice could attend. As the nuns could not travel alone, one of the other Benedictine nuns would come along and become a part of the family for the day.

LuAnn on the swing set

Family Grows;
Life Gets Even Busier

We didn't know at the time but one day a precious little girl was getting ready to join our family. Carolyn Jeanne was born on May 7, 1959 in Albany General Hospital.

I had just a few contractions and then she was born. She

Ellen, Jake, Frank, LuAnn holding Carolyn, and Ric 1959

was a curly-haired beautiful little girl who was very easy to take care of. She had a happy personality and enjoyed whatever her brothers and sisters were doing. She was very easy to entertain and laughed frequently.

With three boys and three girls needing their own bedrooms, we planned out the new arrangement. The boys would have the biggest bedroom. We put the trundle bed in their room. LuAnn and Ellen would share a room, and the baby could be comfortable wherever we put her.

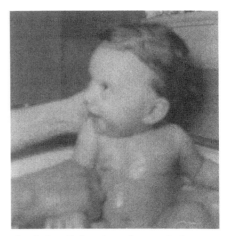

Carolyn's smile has always been contagious.

We took the front bedroom where Ron had slept because he was now in the Navy on assignment. The boys bunking together made sense and worked fine until we realized that Jacob had a strange nighttime ritual that kept the other boys awake. He banged his head against the headboard of his bed.

We moved Jacob into the quietest room so he wouldn't bother the boys. He seemed to sleep very soundly and was raring to go every morning. I just kept an eye on him as he fell asleep because I wanted to check to make sure that the thick blanket I put at the head of his bed stayed where I put it. I didn't want him to hurt himself. I don't remember when he stopped his evening ritual. Evidently, he needed the action to fall asleep.

Our schedule continued: three meals a day, naps as needed, and chores finished as expected. Playtime, depending on the weather, was either inside or outside. In between it all, I had washing and folding and putting away clothes, ironing

LuAnn, Frank, Ric, Jake, Ellen, Carolyn.

and planning meals. There were also pediatrician visits for scheduled inoculations. When Ric started school, our days included parent-teacher meetings and other school related activities.

The children attended church only at an age when they could be good. When there were little ones to take care of at home, Norm would attend one Mass and I would go to another. I usually went early on Sundays as I was awake anyway.

As the kids grew, Norm and I felt like they were ready to go on a trip. We started talking about taking them to

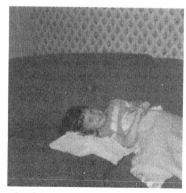

Carolyn.

California so our friends, who had been so kind to us, could meet them.

The summer after Carolyn was a year old sounded like a good time to venture out. Plans included staying in state parks where the bathrooms and shower rooms were available for public use. Norm found a business that rented and sold camping trailers. He found a 16 ft. trailer that had beds on both sides of a center aisle and a bed at the front of the aisle; just what we needed, so he bought it.

Norm signed up for his vacation weeks for July 1960. By that time Carolyn would be fifteen months old.

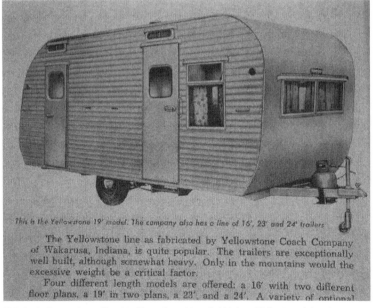

This is the Yellowstone 19' model. The company also has a line of 16', 23' and 24' trailers

The Yellowstone line as fabricated by Yellowstone Coach Company of Wakarusa, Indiana, is quite popular. The trailers are exceptionally well built, although somewhat heavy. Only in the mountains would the excessive weight be a critical factor.

Four different length models are offered: a 16' with two different floor plans, a 19' in two plans, a 23' and a 24'. A variety of optional

This is similar to the trailer that Norm bought, only this is a 19-foot model and ours was 16.*

Trip with Six Children

O ur planning started with "What do we take and what do we leave?"

The 16ft. trailer was parked in our driveway behind the Pontiac station wagon. We began by putting in everything we would need to prepare our meals when we arrived at the campgrounds. (At this time, the fast food restaurants had not been built on every intersection on the highways like we have these days.)

We packed the suitcases with clothes for the sunny weather and planned a change for each child each day. When the morning came for us to leave, we put the high chair, a small potty seat chair, and the playpen down the aisle of the trailer, locked the house up tight, and began our new adventure.

We followed highway 99 south until we reached Medford. Following the road, we turned onto highway 199 through the mountains, stopping to get out and walk around after encountering many curves (car sickness) on the way to the coast and highway 101. Each late afternoon we stopped at the state campgrounds and unpacked the trailer and had an evening meal. The children played under the trees and on play equipment when it was available.

We settled in early, so we could be rested for our journey the next day.

In the morning after breakfast, we continued on highway 101 and enjoyed watching the California ocean surf through the car windows. There were many new sights along the way to keep the children interested and they each excitedly described what they saw. Our first memorable stop came with the large Paul Bunyon statue high above the road. The children were astonished since we had never seen anything that huge.

*Paul Bunyan and Babe, the Blue Ox are in the Redwood Forest and greet people into the Trees of Mystery, a family owned nature attraction. ***

As we drove, the road took us through the trees and fields with herds of deer families in the high grasses. We then saw the giant redwood trees on both sides of the highway. As we drove through, looking for the next campgrounds, we chose a side road into the forest through a water shed of dense trees and thick underbrush.

The forest road narrowed at a small bridge when the back wheel on the right side of the car got stuck. "Where would we find a tow truck out in the forest?" Norm decided to jack up the rear of the car. Everyone got out of the car and stayed in front, out of the way of what might happen on that dangerous highway.

The plan worked, and the tire came forward onto the road. Norm turned around carefully, and we drove onto the road. We all agreed we would not do that again. The next road took us to the correct campground where we spent the night.

We continued with our plans of staying in state parks and driving highway 101 until we turned off onto the road to Los Gatos. We stopped at the appliance store and introduced the children to our friends Mr. and Mrs. Malatesta, visited a while and then drove onto the road to Santa Cruz.

The highway climbs up the hill and at the top, spread out among the trees, is an amusement park with rides for the children named Santa Claus Land. Deer walked in the grassy areas and on the dirt path. The children were amazed that they could touch the deer's hairy bodies and that they didn't frighten the deer away. We have pictures of a large jack-in-the-box and

Largest SANTA CLAUS in the U.S.A.   Santa Claus, Calif.
                                                  via Carpinteria, Calif

Scenes from Santa Claus Land.

a peppermint stick as an example of the other wooden toy structures that were scattered all around the park. We enjoyed experiencing a true children's wonderland. We had seen it so many times when Norm and I lived in Los Gatos because it was right there on the road to Santa Cruz.

After a couple of hours at the park, we continued to the beach town and stopped at the boardwalk in Santa Cruz. We walked along the wooden sidewalk over the ocean and enjoyed the colorful tents where

games were played, and prizes were happy rewards.

We drove south along the beach and took the road to Campbell where our friends, Pat and Ted DeNio lived. We stopped and introduced our friends to the

children. We caught up on what had been happening in their lives and told them all about Norm and his paper mill adventures. After they had a chance to be charmed by the children, we said

our goodbyes and drove back to the campground where the trailer was waiting for us.

We spent several days there before we headed home. As all the clothes were rapidly getting used, we drove into an area of rental cottages and prepared to spend the night. Since a Laundromat was close, we planned to do the wash, so we could have clean clothes and clean diapers on the way back. (Disposable diapers were not on the market at this time.)

After we had our evening meal, we bathed everyone and put them to bed. It had been another exciting day on the road.

Norm and I then had the Laundromat to ourselves, so we used all the washers and dryers. We folded the clean clothes and put them back into the suitcases. We were relieved to have clean clothes again.

Next morning, we were on our way again. We drove inland north on highway 99W until Weed, California and the

Charlotte on the road

intersection with highway 97. We then drove north to Klamath Falls, Oregon.

We continued our plan for a late afternoon stop at a campground and an evening meal, followed by a routine of settling everyone down for the night.

In the morning, we headed west and drove back to Albany. It had been an exciting vacation with new adventures every day, but it was wonderful to get back home. We all decided we needed more space than a 16-foot trailer and a station wagon.

Norm parked the car and trailer in our driveway, got out of the car and ran into the house!!

We all got out of the car, the children ran all around the lawn and to the play structure. Norm came out shouting, "I sold the trailer!" He told us that, before we had left on our trip, a friend told him he wanted a trailer like that and would buy it if Norm decided to sell it. And after that trip, he knew he wanted to sell it. He called the man and sold the trailer.

COME ON----IT WAS A GREAT ADVENTURE---- NO ONE GOT HURT AND WE ALL RETURNED SAFELY....WHAT MORE COULD YOU WANT???????????

We settled back into our lives. If something needed to be done, I would ask one of the kids that was close by to help. Housework seemed to need more than one person to do it all. LuAnn was my helper with folding clean clothes. If she had time she would put the boy's clothes into their dresser drawers. If one of the boys walked by while we were folding, he was given the privilege of putting his and his brother's clean clothes in their dresser drawers.

Registering for school came next on the agenda.

School started in September. Ric was in third grade and LuAnn began grade school. Each weekday morning, the school bus came. The bus stop was beside the road in front of our house. A very patient bus driver brought them back to that same location in the afternoon.

If the weather was agreeable, they could play in the yard before supper. If it wasn't, they had to stay inside, and they had been inside all day. On those days, I let them go out to play as long as they put on their boots and coats.

During the days when things didn't go their way, any child would become unhappy and act up. That happened off and on as any mother can tell you. Sometimes even her most often used methods of distraction would not work, but she would never quit trying.

When the autumn became winter and the skies were usually darkening about 4 P.M, it was easier to have bedtime soon after their warm evening meal. They each brought a book to bed and practiced reading, which pleased a younger sibling who could not read yet. The children were so busy each day that I knew they needed a good night's rest each evening. I always felt that children who learn to be on a schedule know what to expect and are happier.

While I stood cooking hamburgers for supper one day, I realized that I was pregnant. There was something about beef

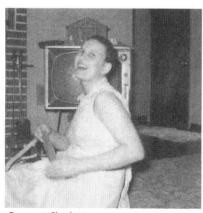

Pregnant Charlotte

that I was sensitive to and I knew immediately why I felt ill. At this time, a new doctor had come to town. His specialization was gynecology and obstetrics. Dr. Glisan was the first doctor with that specialization to set up a practice in Albany. So now I knew who I would be visiting for pre-natal care.

He was a young doctor who had brought his young family to settle in a town that needed a doctor with his specialty. I was one of his first patients and continued regular visits for pre-natal care and delivery. He was an excellent doctor and we were all surprised when, after five years, he announced that he had been hired in a city closer to where he and his wife had grown up.

Another baby to love and so it looked like we were outgrowing our ranch home.

522 West 7th Albany, Oregon

Norm had been looking around downtown Albany for a home for us near church and school. Since school bus trips were so unreliable for the children, and we only had one car for work and the many transportation needs of a growing family, it would be convenient for the children to be able to walk to school each day.

Kids playing in the empty lot next to our house. Our house is in the background.

Desiring help, Norm had spread the word to his friends and co-workers about his search. One day, friend John Bastian told Norm about a large home on Seventh Street near John's family's home. They went to look at it together. Immediately, Norm knew he had found exactly what we needed. A large two-story house plus a basement, a long driveway to the back garage next to the patio, fruit trees and various flowering bushes. The lot was one city block long and ended at the Albany water system canal.

Standing at the end of the lawn, Norm could see a large city playground park on the other side of the canal.

Backyard. Jake, Amy, Sarah, and Donna.

The playground looked close enough for someone to jump across the canal safely. All I saw was a big home that would be a lot of work. But we did need a larger home for our growing family. The location was perfect; four blocks from the church and Catholic grade school; one mile from the town's junior and senior high schools. only a few blocks to the city library, and a few more blocks to the grocery store. We also learned that the hospital was close when the ambulance came screaming by.

Norm told the son of the owner at the real estate company that we wanted to buy the house on Seventh Street. The son said that we should see the inside first and he planned for us to tour the house.

Donna, Ellen, LuAnn, Sarah in front of Ellen, Amy in front of LuAnn.

The steps through the double outside doors led into the glassed-in front porch and to the large oak front door that led into the living room. A piano on the left and an open railing curved staircase with a small leaded glass window on the landing was our first view of the house as we entered. Many windows in the living room and dining room and the tall ceilings welcomed us into the beautiful home. We were impressed that, in the dining room, was a built-in buffet with glass doors and shelves below a large wisteria covered window. The dining room entrance to the kitchen was through a swinging door.

The wall next to the swinging door was filled with a

We put on Christmas plays and other plays in the dining room. We invited friends and family to watch.

mantel-covered fireplace and a small door opening to a narrow staircase which led into a small upstairs bedroom. Next to that door was a larger door leading to a small room with a large closet and a bathroom.

There was a back porch outside the kitchen and small room with steps to the back-yard patio. One kitchen wall had a door to the stairs going to the large basement which had a furnace room, a bedroom with a clothes chute that led from the second floor, and a bathroom and closet under the stairs, a large family room with a pool table, and a laundry room with clothes lines. A few small stairs between the family room and the bedroom led to the driveway outside.

We were also impressed with the second floor and the five bedrooms and a large bathroom with a tub. The owner, Mrs. Tripp, told Norm that there were 3 other families who were interested in buying the house.

After a few days, Mrs. Tripp decided that she wanted us to buy the house because we could raise our family where she and her late husband had raised their family. And so, on December 21, 1960, we signed the papers and purchased the house on Seventh Street, in Albany, Oregon, Linn County.

The Christmas vacation schedule made it convenient to move everything from 2720 South Geary Street to our new home. Ric moved into the bedroom at the north side of the house. Someone (probably [the Tripp's] oldest son) had covered the walls with maps of the world. Someone must have been interested in traveling and the maps fascinated all of us. They were a great addition to our new home. Frank and Jacob moved their belongings into the room at the front of the upstairs. Across from them was the master bedroom for us. LuAnn and Ellen moved into the room across from the bathroom. Carolyn had the small bedroom over the kitchen. We all adapted easily to the extra space in our new home. The children also adapted easily to the neighborhood as many of the students in their school lived nearby. My sisters, Lois and Marlene, and their children, would come to visit for the day every couple of weeks. The cousins played together at the playground and enjoyed their time together planning many projects (that I am just now hearing about).

One time, Marlene brought her clothes that needed to be ironed. So we set up the ironing board in the dining room, got the iron out for her, put on a pot of coffee and spent the afternoon visiting while she worked.

The first summer we were there was a hot one. The upstairs bedrooms were very uncomfortable. Norm purchased a window air conditioner and put it in the upstairs window facing the front of the house. The children brought their blankets to lie on below the window and enjoyed the cool air as they went to sleep.

522 W. 7th Albany, OR

During school, though, this location was so convenient for the children in grade school because they could come home for lunch, reminiscent of my school days when I could eat lunch with Mother and Daddy. It was amazing how fast the mornings went once I became the mother and my children came home for lunch. I remembered saying, as they came in the door with their smiling faces, "Is it lunch time already?"

We found an excellent pediatrician in Albany who wasn't far from the house which made it convenient to keep the inoculation schedule. I also found a very good OB/GYN for my ongoing needs.

A new-to-the-area doctor moved into the offices next to the hospital. Before he came, the only doctors in town were general practitioners. I made an appointment because I knew we were expecting and I needed to continue my check-up visits. One morning in May, it was time to go to the delivery room at the hospital, 4 blocks away.

When Donna was born, the children were so excited to see her that Norm brought them outside the hospital and I held her up to the window so they could see her. Children were not allowed on the maternity floor for some reason.

Baby Donna was a very good baby. Almost too good! She loved to sleep in the bassinette, even with so much noise and commotion going on around her. I remember waking her up so she would be on schedule for nursing and the children wanted to play with her, too.

Carolyn holding Baby Donna

Donna Kathleen was baptized the following Sunday as that was the tradition of our parish: St. Mary's Church. Therefore, the evening before found us polishing shoes and seeing that everyone had something nice to wear to church in the morning.

And our routine continued: school, lunches at home, homework, and then play time after school.

Summers seemed to fly by. Usually we found time while Norm was on vacation from the paper mill to go to the beach or the mountains.

One year, Norm took the children to the Indian Reservation at Kahneeta and they camped and enjoyed the hot springs, at least they said they did. I stayed home with the younger children.

Ric holding Donna. LuAnn to the right.

Usually, at least one snowy day in the mountains found us driving to the summit and the children played in the snow.

Ron and his friend Bob graduated from high school together and decided to join the Navy. They spoke to the Recruiter and Bob was old enough, but Ron wasn't, so I would have to sign the paper giving my permission. After I questioned him to make sure it was really what he wanted, my only concern was that he would regret his decision. My request was that he should never complain to me because I had signed for him to join the Navy. He said he never would (and he never did). For a young teenager who had lost his father before he was three and his mother at 13, this was a very mature decision. I've always been very proud of him.

He entered the Navy on October 3, 1956 and served his promised amount of time. Just as that time was coming to its end, I received a letter from him. It was a request for his money that he had inherited from Mother. He was in Naples, Italy on the S. S. Saratoga Aircraft Carrier and he had agreed to buy an Austin-Healy automobile. (He told me later that salesmen for the company had come on board in Naples, Italy and were selling cars to everyone who wanted one.)

I sent a cashier's check to him because he was sure that was how he wanted to spend his inheritance. Once discharged, he stayed in Florida with the Anderson family. They were friends he had made and they offered their home until he could get settled. He stayed there for two months until the car was delivered to him. Then he drove across the country back to Oregon, 4 years older than when he left. As the GI Bill would pay for his education, he enrolled for classes at Oregon State University. As the other students in his classes were 4 years younger, they acted 4 years younger. Ron stayed for the first term and decided he would do something else.

Something else included Albany city policeman, driving truck for a local beer company, driving the truck, delivering and setting up oxygen containers to patients in their homes or retirement centers.

Ron Schwab

(His work for the Boeing Company in Washington State must have been the most rewarding. His family had a beautiful home in Renton, not far from his work.)

While working during the day, Ron attended night classes and graduated in 1993. Ron married Myrna on January 12, 1963 and they will celebrate their 50th anniversary in their retirement home in Sun City, Arizona on January 12, 2013.

Norm spent his days working off and on in California. When he was sent to New York we were so excited as we were both raised in small towns. He needed a suit and some other casual clothes, so we went shopping. He purchased what he needed, and I suggested he get a hat as business men were wearing

By May, 1962 Donna was walking and talking. She was a very pleasant and agreeable little girl. LuAnn especially enjoyed taking her for a walk.

A neighbor girl, Paula Preston, would come by and ask if she could take Carolyn and Donna to the park to play. If Ellen wasn't already at the park, she went along too.

Ellen, Carolyn, LuAnn with Baby Donna

hats at that time. He told me later that he had set his hat down on a chair and someone sat on it, so he never had a chance to wear it. Hats went out of style about this time, anyway.

The Schmidt family had been having reunions every summer for many years. Sister Bernice and another Sister from the Convent in Mt. Angel would attend the reunion. It was a good way for the family to see Sister Bernice as she had only one day a year to come home. (The family could visit with her at the Convent each month after the yearly restrictions were lifted.) Isabelle usually had the family reunion/picnic at her home in Lebanon. The gathering came to Albany when we had the house with the big back yard.

Happy Donna

There was always a party to go to, either with

LuAnn with Papoose Donna, Jake and Frank in back and Carolyn in front.

family, with church friends, or with Mill friends.

Our Mill friends took turns having parties at their homes and soon our turn came. A special gift that I remember so thankfully was Dee Betts would always stay after the others left and bring the glasses and dishes up to the kitchen from the basement playroom. Then I could do the dishes and clean up easier as everything was in one place.

Being pregnant did not slow me down since there was so much to get done. The next visit to the doctor verified that I was due with number eight in September 1962.

After school had ended in June, the park program began and kept the children of the neighborhood occupied with games and making plans for the end of summer parade.

My sisters and their children continued to come down from their homes in Salem every other week and we all enjoyed

Amy Joan

their visits. The children would play in the yard or at the park. At least once a month someone would try to jump over the canal in the back of the yard and fall in. Through their laughter or tears, we cleaned up the muddy child and then the mess that they brought home.

I enjoyed one night a month attending the parish Catholic Daughters of America meetings and listening to the reports of the charitable events of the previous month. Over the years while we lived in Albany, I served in several offices of the organization. St. Mary's School students had a hot lunch every Thursday which was prepared and served by the Mothers of the students. This was a good way for the Mothers of new students to become acquainted. The other days the children brought their lunches from home.

The Parent's Club and the School Board had their meetings once a month. I served in several of those offices also.

One cool crisp day in late September, Amy Joan was born. When we came home from the hospital, each of the children wanted to hold the new baby. It was my turn when she started to cry because the children couldn't help with her as she was hungry or wet. How could she not be a good child when she got so much attention, and how could she be spoiled since she was a sweet baby and so dearly loved?

Amy was baptized the following Sunday. We went through our regular routine of being sure we had clean clothes and polished shoes ready for church on Sunday.

Everything was going along very well until October 12 and the Columbus Day storm. The winds were howling all around outside the house. Norm was at the Mill. The older children were in school and I was giving Amy a bath in the kitchen sink when the electricity went off. After I wiped her dry, Ric and the other school children came in the door.

School was out, and the teachers were calling parents to come and get their children. There was no way I could leave so I told Ric to go and bring LuAnn home. He said she was helping the teachers. I was so scared that he would get hurt but he was able to bring LuAnn home safely.

I put some hot water from the tap into a pan, so I could warm baby Amy's food. I told the children to go down to the basement, knowing they would be safe there.

I wrapped Amy in a blanket and took her to the basement. Later we saw that the walnut tree in the back yard had fallen over with the roots sticking out of the dirt. The only danger to us inside the house would be if the wind broke a window and we had lots of windows on the main floor. I reasoned that if we all went down to the basement we would be safe, and we did go there for a while, but our curiosity got the better of us and we came upstairs to see what had happened. We had heard a loud noise and saw that the huge pine tree in front of the house had fallen on to the street and into the neighbor's back yard.

Ellen, Amy, Donna, and Carolyn sitting on the front steps of 522 West 7th.

Outside the dining room window, we could see that the pink dogwood tree was leaning over and touching the ground.

Six-year-old Jacob was so upset that he ran from window to window to see what was happening outside. Finally, he put his head into the couch. But that didn't calm him, as the wind was howling and frightening him.

The Columbus Day Storm is considered the benchmark of extratropical wind storms. The storm ranks among the most intense to strike the region since at least 1948, likely since the January 9, 1880 "Great Gale." It's a contender for the title of most powerful extratropical cyclone recorded in the U.S. in the 20th century; with respect to wind velocity, it is unmatched by the March 1993 "Storm of the Century" and the "1991 Halloween Nor'easter" ("The Perfect Storm"). The system brought strong winds to the Pacific Northwest and southwest Canada and was linked to 46 fatalities in the northwest and Northern California resulting from heavy rains and mudslides. *

Jim's Electric

One day, Norm received a phone call from Jim. He owned an electrical contracting business in Lebanon. Jim wanted to talk to Norm about buying his business. So, as Norm felt it was an opportunity he might be interested in, we went to talk to Jim and his wife. Once we arrived and sat in their front room, they seemed to talk about everything else. They talked about when Norm was a boy and wanted to work at the shop. They also talked about people

Family standing in the backyard of 522 West 7th after Ellen's first communion.

they both had known, jobs they had done, who had died and other gossip of a small town. I remember thinking that they would never get to the subject. Finally, Jim asked Norm if he was interested in buying Jim's Electric and Norm said "Yes, how will it be handled?" Then they got down to what Jim had in mind.

Charlotte and Norm with Ellen on her first communion day.

On the way home, I told Norm how frustrated I was that they had taken so long to get to the point. Norm informed me that men did business transactions that way. It was an eye opener for me!

Norm purchased the electrical contracting business and quit the Paper Mill. We decided to stay in Albany since Lebanon was only 15 miles away.

That changed my life. Every Thursday and Friday mornings I put high chair, stroller, and play pen in the station wagon and took 2-year-old Amy and 3-year-old Donna to Lebanon so we could help at the store. We had some walk-in customers but mainly phone calls for emergencies. There were many issues with electrical pumps not working on the farms and homes. The little girls were happy as I brought

Donna and Carolyn

their toys and food for their meals. We had a room where they could nap in the afternoon.

After eight months, Norm received another job offer from Western Kraft. They needed him to go to Kentucky to engineer and build a paper mill in Hawesville. The engineering was to be done in Portland, Oregon and Norm could commute from Albany. After the engineering was complete, Norm would be assigned full time to Hawesville (for about one year) as they built the paper mill. He accepted the job but kept Jim's Electric.

We told the children that Daddy had to go on a job to Kentucky and that he could not go without the family because he would be too lonely without us. So, it was decided that the whole family would go. We assured the children that they could go to schools close to our home. We told them what we knew about the state. Ric remembered that President Lincoln had been born in Kentucky. Little did we know then how much we would eventually learn about Abraham Lincoln.

Norm left for the job site and while he was there he found a house for us in Owensboro. He also checked out the schools. We learned that some of the other engineers and their families from the Albany mill would also be going. Our children had gone to school with their children, so the men who had built the mill in Albany were now assigned to build a paper mill outside the small town of Hawesville, Kentucky. It was about an hour's drive from where we would all live in Owensboro.

The next project was the packing. I gathered all the "baby books" and any other papers that I thought would be needed for the children to register for the school year. Ric 13, would be in high school. LuAnn 11, Frank 10, Jacob 9, Ellen 7, and Carolyn 6, would all be in grade school. My helpers at home were Donna 4, and Amy 3.

We did not take any furniture because we were to select what we would need from a local furniture and appliance store in Owensboro. We became very good friends with the owner and staff of that store. Each child either had a suitcase or shared one for their clothing. As everyone dressed nicely when they flew on an airline in the 60's, we selected our Sunday best, polished our shoes etc., and were all ready to leave the next morning. Each child also took along a game or coloring book or books to read etc. to keep them occupied on the plane.

As some of the airlines were on strike, we followed the news closely. We had the schedule and the tickets, so we knew when we were to leave and arrived at the airport in plenty of time. Everyone was so excited. We boarded the first-class section and settled ourselves in for a great adventure.

Our destination was to be Louisville, Kentucky. Our family had been very interested in the NASA rocket programs as shown on the television, so when 3-year-old Amy was all belted in and the plane took off, she called out, "blast off!" causing many chuckles. The pilot flew from Portland, Oregon to San Francisco, California and landed. Then we flew on to Dallas, Texas and landed. We were to change planes there, so we got off. (I remember the humidity was something I have never encountered.) We climbed the steps into the lobby and waited for the next plane. Whenever we entered a different plane, the pilots and stewardesses gave miniature pilot wings to each of the children. They took time to talk to them and asked if there was anything they needed. As each child had brought something to entertain themselves, they didn't need anything else and said thank you to each concern. Our next flight took us to Atlanta, Georgia then to Louisville, Kentucky.

The plane landed in a storm. The thunder was deafening, and the lightening hit the wing of the plane as we landed. No damage was done to the plane, so everyone got off safely. We waited to be the last to leave because it took a while to collect all the things that had been brought on board.

As a station wagon was waiting for us, we started the drive to Owensboro and our new home.

*

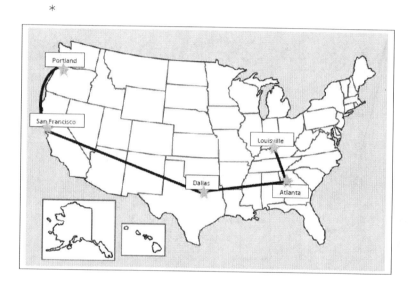

A Note from Amy

To quote my mom who was flying with eight children and her husband: "The pilot flew from Portland, Oregon to San Francisco, California and landed. Then we flew on to Dallas, Texas and landed. We were to change planes there, so we got off. I remember the humidity was something I have never encountered. We climbed the steps into the lobby and waited for the next plane. […] Our next flight took us to Atlanta, Georgia then to Louisville, Kentucky." Above is the flight we took when I was super eager to "Blast Off!" Can you even imagine a trip like that alone, much less with eight children 13-years and under? And then be struck by lightning?

Adventures In and Around
Owensboro, Kentucky

We arrived the summer of 1965. After selecting furniture and settling into our new home, we explored the neighborhood. Grocery stores, schools, church, play areas, and whatever we needed, had to be close since we would be without a car. We had the station wagon, but it was also a company car for the men to travel to the future mill site in Hawesville; an hour away. During the day, another family who had also moved from Albany helped us when we needed transportation.

Our days were busy registering for schools, both grade and high. We were welcomed wherever we went, and we soon learned that "southern hospitality" was not an empty phrase. The Kentuckians have a charming accent and many times they would ask us what our accent was. We always replied that we did not have an accent. They assured us that we did.

When another mom and I registered the younger children in the Catholic grade school, we discovered they had a hot lunch program each day and we were asked which day we could help. We chose Wednesday. We had already planned, along with the other wives from Albany, to take every Thursday and explore areas outside the city and include lunch along the way. Sometimes we had a car full and other times we had two cars full of inquisitive women and some small children who came along.

When we came back to the "hot lunch" program the following Wednesday we were bombarded with questions as to where we went and what we did. Many of the places we had explored were no more than an hour or two away from the city and we were surprised when the native Kentuckian women said they had never been there.

One Saturday morning, Jacob and Frank decided that they wanted to make a model airplane. The only store that sold models was in another neighborhood. As they walked, they noticed a group of boys playing a game. They were surprised as the boys had dark skin. They continued their way to the store and back. They mentioned where they'd been. I was curious to how far they had gone. One Saturday I took them in the car to the model shop as they needed something else. As we came to an intersection and stopped for the red light I asked if that was where the black children lived, and they said "Yes." As I looked around I saw many trees and shrubs and small houses. In Oregon we lived in a town with only one black family and they owned a business. This would be the first time the little boys had seen a neighborhood where black families lived.

As a family, every Sunday after mass, we would explore Owensboro and the areas that were within driving distance. An interesting area outside the city was where the coal mines were located. One area we especially enjoyed had a "big shovel." We were fascinated by the size of the equipment that they used to dig into the surface of the earth. We have pictures of all the children standing in the huge bucket.

We treasured that experience of seeing something we would never see in Oregon.

Another trip on a Sunday took us to where the Ohio River flows into the Mississippi River. The Mississippi River is silt-colored, and the Ohio River is clear. It was very interesting for all of us to see the waters mix together.

Owensboro, located on the banks of the Ohio River, is

Carolyn, Donna, and Amy.

the largest city in eastern Kentucky. A huge bridge connects the interstate highway to Indiana. We learned that each farmer had a tobacco allotment from the federal government. As we drove through the countryside, we saw a section of each farm where tobacco was growing. This tobacco was harvested and then dried in the warehouses. After it dried, auctioneers with their loud encouraging voices could be heard selling the crops.

There were three distilleries in the city; Makers Mark, Seagrams, and Jack Daniels. Large warehouses were used to house the barrels that age the liquor.

Two weeks before Christmas, Chris, one of the wives from Albany, found a recipe for bourbon balls. She suggested we get together and make some of the candy and send boxes of them back home as Christmas gifts. As we were always looking for something different to do, we willingly agreed.

Chris bought the ingredients and we all gathered in her kitchen, planned where we would send the gifts, set everything on the table and proceeded to have fun. No, we did not drink any of the excellent local bourbon until the boxes were all ready to go to the post office.

On a snowy morning, December 10, 1966, Sarah Jane was born. She had curly black hair and a loud cry. She was welcomed into the world of brothers and sisters.

I had her first name chosen but was searching for a second name to go with Sarah. A friend came to visit and wanted me to name her Dixie. It just did not fit so she suggested a

---

Kentucky Bourbon Balls

Ingredients
1 cup pecans or walnuts
¾ cup bourbon, divided
2 cups crushed graham crackers or Nilla Wafers
¼ cup Dutch-process cocoa powder, divided
¼ cup confectioners' sugar, divided
¼ cup light corn syrup

Directions
1. In a small bowl, combine the nuts and ¼ cup of the bourbon. Cover with plastic wrap and let sit 2 to 3 hours.
2. In a large mixing bowl, combine all ingredients.
3. Using a heaping tablespoon portion, roll dough into ¾-inch balls.
4. In a separate bowl, combine ¼ more cocoa powder and ¼ more confectioners' sugar and coat balls in the cocoa sugar. Transfer to parchment-lined baking sheet.
5. Cover and chill for at least 2 hours or until firm.

nickname. I tried it out many times, but she was a Sarah, a beautiful curly haired gentle, sweet little girl. When we brought her home, everyone wanted to hold her. She was well-taken-care-of and the only rule was that she could not be held "all the time."

The trips with the ladies to see the area went by the wayside. They went on without me and I heard of all the new places they saw and the pleasant lunches in the new towns. Sometimes another mom from Albany, Shirley Kasparek, who had a youngster the same age as Amy, would let her daughter come to play and stay the day. Then all the moms returned with stories of their adventure.

On Christmas Day 1966, Sarah Jane was baptized in Immaculate Conception Church in Owensboro, Kentucky. Her godparents were Ted and Shirley Kasparek. Their children, and many other friends, celebrated the occasion with our family.

As we entered the church most of the lights had been turned off in the cathedral. The trees around the baptismal font were brightly lit with many red, green, and white lights.

It was truly a blessed occasion. When the priest poured the holy water on her forehead, Sarah's reaction was loud and echoed to the ceilings. Then the echoes came from the laughter of the children.

I remember "back to school" nights, well baby visits to the doctor, children making angel wings in the snow, going out for a walk on a sunshiny morning in a single digit cold day, and the trips after church on Sundays to explore the countryside.

As with any family, everywhere we went we found a new adventure. Late one afternoon, we heard on the radio that a tornado was expected in our county. The sky was dark blue with flashes of lightening and noisy thunder. As we went up to the large bedroom on the second floor of the house and watched out the window, we saw billowing clouds with balls of lightening shooting out of the sky that appeared to be behind the clouds. The lightning seemed to have changing colors of blues and reds. The next day we discovered that there had been a tornado not far from our home.

When school was over, we planned to drive the nine-seat station wagon back to our home in Oregon since Norm was finished with his job in Kentucky. As we had explored many of the sites where Abraham Lincoln had lived in Kentucky, we planned to follow the Lincoln Trail so we could use our trip back home as a learning experience for the children. Our interest about this important time in history began when we saw the rustic birthplace of Abraham Lincoln in our weekly explorations while living in Owensboro.

We planned our trip back home on the maps we acquired of the Lincoln Trail and of the US. Our first long stop would be in Springfield, Illinois and the Capitol building.

As we traveled the United States, always going west, we stopped at many of the Capitol buildings of the states where we were spending the night. Our driving time each day began after a good breakfast at the Holiday Inn and ended each day around 3 or 4 P.M. so the children could swim in the pool before supper and bed time at the next Holiday Inn.

At this time, the Holiday Inn Corporation was focused on hospitality and each employee made it very comfortable for us with their many kindnesses. The other couples traveling that summer were also kind to the children and many times a friendly lady would want to hold the baby so I could eat my breakfast.

Our first view of Oregon was the Eastern side of Mt. Hood and then we really got excited.

The Schmidt family in 1968.
Back row: Ric, Charlotte, Sarah and Norm
Middle row: LuAnn, Frank, Jake, Ellen
Front: Donna, Amy, Carolyn

Camp Odor Socks

When we were still living in Kentucky and making our plans to return to Oregon, the boys came home from school with information about a summer camp for boys that would start a week after the end of school. The scheduled stay would be two weeks.

Camp Ondessonk was located in southern Illinois. Ondessonk is a Huron Indian tribe name meaning "Bird of Prey."

Assigned parents transported the boys to the camp and other parents would drive to pick them up after the allotted two-week stay. The boys had a wonderful time. They returned with their suitcases full of the dirtiest clothes I had ever seen and stories about their adventures.

Each group of boys was given the name of an Indian tribe and a shirt with the color of their group. It was a comfortable method for the younger boys to know where they needed to be. All the games were lessons on the Indian heritage.

The large campground consisted of a recreation room, a mess hall, a chapel and cabins with bunk beds. They were all among the Sugar Maple and Swamp Cypress trees adjacent to the Shawnee National Forest of Southern Illinois.

The boys learned how to swim, how to row a boat, how to row a canoe, and how to ride a horse.

As the older boys had an area of their own where they slept in tree houses, screened wooden barracks, or a cliff house that looked down on the river, the younger boys never saw them until it was time for the journey back home.

Ric and Jake in the back yard, Albany, OR

After all their tasks had been finished, it was the day of their final activity: graduation. It was held in a large natural circular rock amphitheater.

When the boys reminisced about their two weeks of adventures they began calling the camp by the name Camp "odor socks." Remembering their clothing that they had brought back, the new name wasn't far from the truth.

Home Sweet Home; Tell City, Indiana

Our neighbors and friends welcomed us back to Albany. They had put a large Welcome Back poster on the house.

We introduced our Kentucky Babe, Sarah Jane, to everybody in our small community. At seven months, she was delighted with all the attention.

We stepped back into our lives in our home. The summer included medical and dental checkups for everyone. Much work needed to be done in the house that had not been lived in for a year. We enjoyed meeting new neighbors that had moved into the neighborhood since we had been gone.

The kids played with their neighborhood friends at our city park (Henderson Park) that was located behind our house and on the other side of the canal. When Carolyn played on the swings at the park, she would sing out "Fly in the Sky" only she would pronounce the words the way she had learned them in Kentucky and it came out "Fla Ha in the ska." The children wanted her to get rid of her southern accent, but I said, "Let her alone. She will get over it when she goes back to school and hears the teachers talk."

During the summer, each park in Albany had a college student from the city in charge of games and playground supplies. These programs were a wonderful way for the children to meet each other and have a safe place to play. If it rained, they would have their classes under the picnic tables. All the neighborhood children had a fun-filled summer vacation as they played the games and created crafts and costumes. In August, they all participated in a parade downtown showing the costumes they had made.

Norm went back to work and brought home different rumors that were circulating about another mill being built next to the one that they had just finished in Kentucky.

We were told that a bridge from Hawesville, Kentucky to Canellton, Indiana was being built. This would make it easier for the engineers from the headquarters office in Portland to get to the mill site. The closest airport to the mill site was Evansville, Indiana. With a bridge, they would no longer have to take the ferry across the Ohio River between Kentucky and Indiana.

The company decided that Norm would be needed to help build the mill in Indiana and to be in charge of the electrical and instrumentation installation.

As Norm could not be close-by for advice and the running of his electrical contracting business in Lebanon: Jim's Electric, he decided to find a partner for the business. He chose an electrician friend who lived in the same town who would be available to oversee everything.

We were all set to move for a year to Tell City, Indiana.

Tell City;
Number Ten is Born

Our move to Indiana was similar to our move to Kentucky. However, our flight from Portland to Evansville was not as complicated as the flight to Louisville. We arrived in Evansville in the evening of a warm day in August 1968. The long flight was tiring and the car ride to Tell City was even more tiring.

It was a long day for everyone. A friend told Norm that the Postmaster in Tell City had purchased an old house and had fixed it up for a family to live in. That was the house we rented and were very thankful for. Some very kind friends knew what furniture we would need and set the house up enough so we could get settled for our first night there. It was very much welcomed because we were all exhausted.

The heat of Indiana was different than what we were used to in Oregon and baby Sarah, now 20 months old, suffered. She couldn't feel comfortable in the heat. And even to this day she suffers when it gets too hot.

Six months later our Martha Joy arrived on January 12, 1969. What a joy she was and continues to be to this day! Always active, always inquisitive, always learning. Her eyes would follow all the children around as they continued their active lives and Martha watched.

Charlotte with Martha and Ric. 522 W 7th St. Albany, OR

When the older children began to go off to college, Martha cried. She was so sad to see her siblings leave. We explained to her that they would be back, but she felt such great sadness when they left.

And then, when they came back, she sat in their laps and cuddled with them as much as she could until they had to go back to school again. She also learned their tricks early in life. When they asked her to get a cookie or something from the kitchen while they sat watching TV, she would bargain with them: "I'll do it for a quarter." And, if it was important enough for them, they would pay it. Or they would promise to pay it and never actually pay it. Martha knew who she could bargain with and who she couldn't. She knew who would pay her for her errands and who wouldn't. She has always had a great mind for numbers.

Our Purchase

Or

One of the Interesting Brainstorms That We Had

As our home base was Albany, Oregon, and it had been since 1955, we started discussing where we would retire when Norm's electrical engineering career came to an end. Back in Albany after one year in Indiana, Norm read an ad in the local newspaper. It said that a downtown hardware store was for sale and he thought it sounded interesting. He called the phone number and who should answer but Hillman, an acquaintance from our parish church. Hillman was handling the sale for the owner as he lived out of town.

Albany Farm Supply building is now the Albany Historical Museum

Norm was excited to find out that the store for sale was Albany Farm Supply. He knew the store, having been a customer for a number of years. After talking to Hillman and meeting the owner, he had gotten all the information he needed to figure out what it would take to buy one of his favorite stores. It was a great way to plan for his retirement.

Norm had always been a "Jack of all trades" and could fix anything. Thus, in 1970, we purchased a neighborhood hardware store that supplied the needs of the local farmers and various industries in the valley.

Albany Farm Supply was definitely a man's store. If a woman came in the door, she probably had a list of items her husband or boss needed, and they knew that the clerks would help her. The clerks would know what the item was and where it was located inside the store. They would fill her list to her boss's satisfaction.

When Norm purchased the store, everything came with it including the stock and the store's manager. Except for the building. We had to pay rent on the two-story old, wooden building with wooden floors that was built in 1898. The main floor had the merchandise for sale and upstairs was extra supplies and shelves. The ladders were stored there as were less popular items.

The building was owned by a family trust administered by a local elderly lawyer whose office was around the corner on First Street. Mr. Weatherford was the last remaining member of a prestigious family who owned other downtown buildings.

After we had been paying rent for a number of years, Norm asked me to ask Mr. Weatherford if we could buy the building. The next morning, I went around the corner and through the front door of another old building. As I entered, he was sitting behind an antique desk that must have been either an expensive purchase or a family heirloom. He asked me to be seated in an old wooden chair in front of the desk.

I explained our request for the purchase of the building.

Without hesitation, he said "No." When I asked him why, he said, "Just because we want to pay it off first."

Sassy me said, "You should have had it paid off with all the rent you've been getting for all these years."

So he said, "We spent that money on other things and will not sell it to you."

And here I thought lawyers were business people too.

The King Sisters Contest

While watching the Lawrence Welk show last Saturday night, one of the precious memories of the past came to me. The King Sisters. Our family enjoyed the King Sisters television show that had a large orchestra. We loved listening to the sisters harmonize as they sang, orchestra music playing in the background. The only TV we had was in the living room and only turned on for special shows. As I enjoyed the harmony of the sisters, I always watched the show.

The King Sisters got their start on the Lawrence Welk Show.

As the years went on, their daughters were included in the programs. A classical guitarist, husband of one of the sisters, fascinated me. I did not realize that the guitar was that adaptable. During a break in the show, usually used for commercials, the announcer said we could enter a contest and receive a key to a car that was being donated by a local dealer. To enter: write a letter to the address shown and tell us what you enjoyed about the show. That sounded like a fun challenge to me.

Since the show came on after our evening meal, the children would take their baths, put on their pajamas in preparation for bed and come into the living room ready to enjoy the music together. Having our routine in mind, I wrote to the station manager, told them all about us. Later we received a letter with a key explaining the contest rules. We were invited to bring the key and arrive at the studio auditorium Saturday afternoon before 4:00 P.M.

We made plans to stay the night in Portland. We were all excited, packed our clothes for the next day, and looked each other over carefully. When we were satisfied that we all looked our best, we scrambled into the station wagon and started our fun journey seventy miles to Portland.

All the contestants and their families gathered in the TV studio auditorium. We could see the bright, shiny new car on the stage. You could feel the excitement when we entered the auditorium. As each number was called, each contestant came on stage and tried their key in the car. Each time the engine did not turn on, everyone said, "Oh, oh, oh!!" Disappointed for that person.

When my number was called, I was so excited that I don't remember walking to the stage. I do remember putting my key in and being surprised that nothing happened. I could hear the "oh, oh, oh."

Yes, someone else had the right key. We clapped and were happy for them.

We all enjoyed the contest and continued to watch our favorite Saturday evening show.

Our Albany

Our days were busy in our big home in Albany. The children were always going here and there and so was I. I volunteered with Loaves and Fishes, served on the PTA at St. Mary's Catholic School, and was involved in church groups.

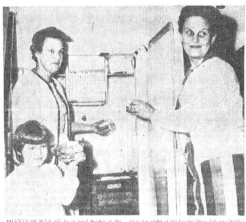

Newspaper article: Mrs. McCafferty is handing Carolyn a carton of milk. Charlotte on the right.

The children went to St. Mary's for 1st grade through 6th grade. They then went to Junior High School at Memorial Junior High that was from 7th grade to 9th grade. Then on to West Albany High School for 10th, 11th and 12th grade. When the children went to

St. Mary's, they walked to school and went directly into the church for daily mass as every day began with daily mass. I sometimes joined when the baby was ready for the day.

When they went to junior high and high schools, they walked the one mile to school.

Charlotte in front of St. Mary's Catholic Church after Leslie Schwab, Ron and Myrna's daughter, was baptized. Janelle, Ron and Myrna's first born, is to Charlotte's right.

Once the children were old enough to work, they got jobs. Before Carolyn started working at Fred Meyer, she worked on the accounts at the Albany Farm Supply. She helped our accountant who was my cousin Larry's wife, Carolyn Schwab. (Carolyn and Carolyn still have a close bond because of the time they spent going over the accounts.) As we extended credit to all the businesses in the community, it was a big job sending out monthly bills to everyone. These days you would pay with your VISA credit card, but in those days people would say, "Put it on my bill." And we would. Every month we sent out many, many invoices to be paid in 30 days. And every month people paid their bills. Mostly in 30 days but some businesses and farming businesses would need a little bit more time. When that happened, we would charge them interest. Our community counted on us to be there, extending credit and providing them with what they needed at a fair price. And we counted on them to buy from us and pay on time.

Ellen was not only the first female newspaper "boy" for the Albany Democrat Herald, but she was also our first female sales clerk at Albany Farm Supply. In 1971, she started clerking and putting up with the men's jokes and tricks. Nobody wanted her to wait on them until they found out she could find anything in that store. She proved to them that girls can do whatever boys can do because when tested, she knew right

Charlotte conversing with a leadership group of volunteers from different churches.

where everything was. There were so many items that were stuck in every nook and cranny that a person always needed a clerk to tell them where anything was.

Donna worked in the store, too. She worked there for many years as a clerk. Norm and I always believed that what the boys could do, the girls could also do.

Amy babysat a lot and worked in a church nursery. A pastor from another denomination had asked our priest if we had any good babysitters and he thought of our family. I asked Amy if she was interested and she was very much interested. She also worked at the little mini mall down by the Farm Supply that had little shops that sold many things. The store she worked in sold dance clothes like leotards and ballet slippers.

The boys worked at a flower greenhouse delivering flowers to the ladies of the town. Boy did those ladies love getting their flower deliveries when they saw those handsome boys deliver them!

The children were always involved in either seeing me volunteer with many church and community activities or volunteering too. The boys were involved in Search and Rescue. They went through training and saved some stranded people in the wooded areas around Linn County. When a Search and Rescue job turned into a "recover" job, that was the worst part of the job.

They also picked strawberries for many, many summers. Ask them all about their picking days. About the early mornings, the bus rides, the red stained fingers when they came home, the loads and loads of wash, the hot sun beating down, the friends they met, the laughter, and the tons and tons of red, sweet berries that they picked to make money for college and other things. They would probably say that it was the worst job in the world and the best one, too.

522 West 7th Street
Albany, Oregon 97321
926-6400

Norm and I always felt that we made the right decision when we moved back to Oregon. As soon as we moved to Albany, we felt a part of the community.

Our house at 522 West 7th Street was large, and just the right size for us. There was always something to do around the house. Chores were a constant with the girls helping me out on the inside and the boys helping Norm out on the outside. There were always more kids around the house than just our

Our Albany home: 522 W. 7th.

10 as the children had many friends and our house was the fun house on the block.

At dinnertime, you could hear mothers calling to their children to come in for dinner. I would yell, "Schmidt kids! Dinner!"

As the evening hours in the summertime were the most fun for the kids to play at the park, I found myself yelling, "Schmidt kids! Time to come in!" every night at dusk.

The younger kids liked putting on plays. Donna, Amy, Sarah, and Martha would entertain anyone who wanted to watch their performance. The main dining room of our house

Donna, Amy, Carolyn.
Sarah and Martha in front.

had a sliding wooden door that blocked the dining room off from the front room. They would use that as a stage curtain and the dining room as their stage. They put on Christmas plays, plays that they wrote, and plays that they found in library books. Sometimes the neighborhood ladies would come to watch.

During summer when Ellen and Carolyn worked at the Farm Store, they would come home for lunch. At that time, All My Children, the soap opera, played at noon. As soon as Ellen got her sandwich she sat on the couch to eat and watch the show. Every day she said, "What did I miss?" And the other girls would explain to her what she missed. All the while missing what was happening at that moment. We all liked Erica Cain and wondered what she was going to do next.

The washers and dryers were in the basement in the furnace room. There had been an old furnace down there to heat the house in the past, but we had an electric furnace. The old furnace was still there, and we could burn garbage if we wanted to. We did sometimes. I had two washers and two dryers in the laundry room. I also had lines made of wire to hang wet laundry. The sheets and some clothes were always hung to dry. But the towels and jeans and other clothes were always put in the dryers. I also ironed in that room or in the dining room off the kitchen where we all ate. We had a long table in that room with a bench on one side and chairs on the other. There was enough room for all 12 of us to sit at that table for our meals.

We had two telephones. One was upstairs in our bedroom and one was on the wall in the kitchen with a long windy cord. Many times, when the girls had boyfriends, they would sit in the doorway between the kitchen and the dining room, holding the phone to their ears or pulling that cord as far away from the phone as they could

The dining room was always a gathering place: Martha, Carolyn, someone's college friend, Amy (probably), another college friend, Donna (probably), LuAnn, Ellen.

to get the privacy that they wanted. When they had been on the phone long enough I would say, "Get off that phone. You've been on it long enough!"

Louisiana

In 1973, three years after we got back from Indiana, we were off again. This time we would live in Natchitoches, Louisiana. The mill was located in Campti, a small town on the eastern bank of the Red River. The company families, though, lived in townhouses on the Cane River in the quaint town of Natchitoches.

Norm bought a boat and taught the girls how to waterski. Even 5th grader Amy learned how. She would put our only ski vest on, an adult size, and get lost in the jacket. We called her the headless skier when she was down in the water as the large ski jacket floated way above her head. Norm and Ellen learned how to slalom ski by starting out with 2 skis and dropping one half-way down the river. Sarah and Martha were too young to ski, but they loved being the lookouts. Someone had to watch the skier while Norm or Ellen drove the boat.

The children all went to the Catholic school as it had grades kindergarten through 12th grade. We felt right at home because that school was also called St. Mary's just like in Albany. The people were very friendly and we all made friends very quickly.

At that time, Ric, LuAnn, and Frank were in college. Ric and LuAnn had chosen to apply to Oregon State University in Corvallis, Oregon, a 20-minute drive from Albany. Frank attended University of Oregon in Eugene as they had the best school of architecture. Jacob was a senior in high school and wanted to graduate at West Albany High School where all his friends were going, so he lived his senior year with our neighbors in Albany, the Boock family. Johnny Boock and Jake had always been great friends, so he and his wife Mary were happy to open their home to our almost 18-year-old.

We lived there, on the banks of Cane River, for one school year and then went back to our home in Albany. The Albany house hadn't been lived in all year, so the boys and Norm cleaned it up to get it ready for us to return.

Martha and Sarah with our Louisiana Christmas tree.

Three years later, we returned to Natchitoches for another school year as Norm needed to fulfill more responsibilities at the mill in Campti. It was 1976 so the only girls who came with us were the last four: Donna, Amy, Sarah, and Martha. It was Carolyn's turn to be a senior and she also wanted to graduate from West Albany High School where her friends were. This time, we thought it was a good idea to bring a family into our home to rent it while we were gone. That way they could take care of it and it wouldn't sit empty. We met a family through my brother Ron and his wife Myrna. Since they were friends of my family, we felt that our Carolyn could stay living in her bedroom while attending school and working at Fred Meyer. She was a very responsible young lady.

While she lived there, she wasn't our main concern. The family living there were smokers and they were our main concern as they didn't keep up our home as we would expect them to. They were also very loud and disturbed our poor Carolyn to a point that she had to move out. She spent the rest of her senior year living with some very good friends, the Hubert family, who lived only two blocks away. Mr. and Mrs. Hubert were very kind to our Carolyn and she was so happy to be away from the smoke and the noise.

While in Louisiana, the girls made lots of friends. So many that they were given "going away parties" when we left at the end of the year. By that time, the girls had thick southern accents and deep dark tans from the sun and swimming and water skiing. Living on the river was nice as we had returned to the same townhouses that we had stayed in the first time we had lived there.

When we came home, our house was sparkling clean. The boys, Norm, and the girls who were still in Oregon spent hours on their hands, knees, and ladders cleaning everything. The smell of smoke and the thick grey film that had settled on the walls and windows from the cigarettes were cleaned so thoroughly that the only thing left from that family who had taken over our house was the few Amway products they had left under our sink.

Now that the girls had many friends in Louisiana, they had pen pals that gave them stories of what was happening in Natchitoches while we were in Oregon. We exchanged Christmas cards with many of our friends from Natchitoches and continue to keep our friendships with these very loving people. Amy missed her friends so much that she traveled to Natchitoches the summer after her 9th grade year. She stayed with our friends the Lovell's and with her friend from St. Mary's. And after all these years, our fond memories of time spent in Natchitoches is always pleasant and happy. And when we really miss it, we can watch the movie Steel Magnolias and the views from Natchitoches can be remembered with a smile.

First Signs of Gray Hair

I knew that I would eventually have gray hair because my father's hair started to become gray among his black, curly hair.

So, there they were, my first gray hairs!

Until the gray became noticeable, I told the beautician that I wanted it covered up. I still had children in grade school and I didn't want them asked about their grandmother!!!

Thus, I had lovely thin brown hair for many years, with the weekly help of a beautician.

Then we lived in Kentucky where the current style was backcombing the hair, so it was high on the head. Oh, we thought we were so beautiful! Recently I saw a picture of myself with the "high hair"! It looked terrible!

Charlotte

As my hair got grayer and grayer, it came to the point that the beautician told me she just couldn't hide the gray any longer. By this time, I had become accustomed to the fact that

I would have gray hair whether I liked it or not. So, with the help of the beautician's magic, eventually all the dark coloring faded or grew out.

Now, with weekly visits to the beauty parlor, the color has become very comfortable. Until

Charlotte and Donna before her First Communion

recently, I thought everyone became gray as they aged…but apparently not…as once in a while someone will stop me and say they like the gray and share that their hair will never get gray.

Moving to Portland

In 1979, Norm was offered a job with a new company: Willamette Industries. He had been working for Western Kraft for years, owning his own businesses (Albany Farm Supply and Jim's Electric) for years, and now his hard work was paying off. Although he didn't want to take the job, he was hesitant as it meant he would have to uproot his family and move permanently to Portland, Oregon. They made the offer again. He turned it down again. His expertise was what they needed for their business and they knew his worth because they had worked with him at Western Kraft. When he turned it down the second time it was because he wasn't confident it would stick around as it was a business that was just starting out. You can't raise a family on an income that may or may not be solid. Who knew if the company would make it? Western Kraft was a sure thing. Willamette Industries wasn't.

And then they called him a third time. He said to me, "If I tell them that I'll work for them only if they pay me a lot of money, they'll leave me alone. There would be no way that they would pay me what I ask for because it would be way too big. Then they'll leave me alone."

He made his offer. They countered his offer with twice what he asked for, making him an offer he couldn't refuse. So he agreed. For many years he drove back and forth from Albany to Portland to fulfill his obligations to the company. He didn't want to uproot his family if the company wasn't a sure thing. If they went out of business and he had moved his family to Portland, it would be terrible. We wouldn't survive. It was difficult on him, but after a few years we realized that this company was making it. The people were reliable. He had already known them for years, anyway, because they had gotten their start at Western Kraft.

So we sold our beautiful, historical house and bought a house in Portland and moved. It wasn't like the year jaunts we had made to Kentucky, Indiana, and Louisiana. This was a permanent move.

Amy was a junior in high school and Donna was a senior. It was now Donna's turn to stay in Albany and graduate from West Albany High School with all her friends, just like her brother Jake had, and her sister Carolyn. The Boock family, once again, opened their home to one of our children. We left Albany in November, after the first 9 weeks of school had already begun.

Amy was in high-steppers in Albany, a dance/drill team, and she was sad to have to leave. I found out about the dance team at her new Portland high school, Andrew Jackson High School, and contacted their choreographer/teacher. She tried out for their dance team, mid-year, and was accepted. She had already made a friend, even before starting school there as they had met at her tryouts. Whenever we moved in the past, she always had her big sister Donna right by her side to lean on. This time, she had to navigate school alone. Sarah and Martha attended the local Catholic school that had K-8th grade. Sarah was in 6th grade and Martha was in 5th.

Portland high schools were different than what we were used to. In Albany, Owensboro, and Tell City we were always close enough for the children to walk to school as we lived a few miles away at the most. In Portland, I had to drive the children to school. The high school was miles away, but the school buses were only in service to bus students from Northeast Portland. At that time, the communities who lived in Northeast Portland were predominantly made up of African Americans. The busing system that was set up in this way was done to give those children the same opportunities as the children in Southwest Portland, an area that was made up of communities that were predominantly Caucasian. So, since the buses were already full, they didn't pick up any students from our area. Parents and children with driver's licenses had to drive to school. The Jackson High School student parking lot was always full of cars as most students just drove themselves. Once Amy felt comfortable driving a stick shift car into the busy streets of Portland, she, too, drove herself to school.

The house we bought was a modern design, completely different than our home in Albany. We had a hot tub in the basement. It had been a house that was in one of the first "Street of Dreams" neighborhoods in Portland. Back when they weren't as elaborate as they are now-a-days.

Charlotte with Sarah and Martha

By this time, Jacob had attended Linn Benton Community College in Albany and OSU in Corvallis, Ellen went to U of O in Eugene, and Carolyn went to OSU. Donna was on track to attend OSU for teaching. Our big family was finding their way in the world as they all got bachelor's degrees and went on to careers. A few were waylaid along the way for a short time, but always seemed to find their way back to a definite future.

Schmidt Hardware

In 1982/83 Norm decided to purchase a hardware store in Salem. We had already owned Albany Farm Supply for ten years and it was doing very well. The Salem store got the name Schmidt Hardware. Norm was working 50-60 hours a week for Willamette Industries, so he needed me to help him much like I had done at Jim's Electric. But this time, I didn't have any little children to come help. Amy had already graduated from Jackson High School and Sarah and Martha were 15 and 13 years old.

As we were trying to cut back on overspending, but still needed to replenish inventory, I didn't want to spend too much time with salespeople. The particularly difficult ones still had to be dealt with, so I put in a special system. When they called, I told them my name was Rita. When they called back and asked for Rita, the guys told them they had the wrong number. So ended my dealing with that salesman.

I worked in both Albany and Salem, driving my yellow Ford Ranchero back and forth on I-5 every Monday through

Friday. There were times when I stayed the night with Lois in Salem, so I didn't have to drive all the way back to Portland just to turn around and go back to Salem. Those times were filled with fond memories as Lois always made me laugh. Many times, her children visited so we talked about memories from the past. Little did I know when I worked in the dry cleaners or the soda shop back before I was married, that I would be working at a hardware store, in Salem, in the future.

Eventually, soon after I started working at both stores, Norm hired his brother Larry to manage Albany Farm Supply and he hired our new son-in-law Fred, married to Ellen, to manage Schmidt Hardware. But I still worked hard at keeping everything organized and running smoothly. I did this job for a few years until we sold Albany Farm Supply to a very nice man who loved the business as much as we did. And we liquidated Schmidt Hardware. By this time, many of our children had married wonderful spouses and the miracle of birth was starting to create the next generation.

Albany Farm Supply is now Albany Regional Museum and can be visited Tuesday through Saturday. Their displays are wonderful and really give an accurate historical representation of Albany's history.

part three

The Retirement Years

China and Hong Kong

Under cloudy skies we boarded United flight 1157 on April 22, 1989 at 10:55am. Our seats were 2C and 2D. By 12:45pm we had arrived in San Francisco, sunny and beautiful as usual. We sat on the comfy couches in the International lounge where we heard many languages spoken and saw many nationalities until flight 805 boarded at 1:23pm. Our first-class seats were roomy and comfortable. They offered us champagne and orange juice. It was a long trip and we crossed the dateline somewhere along the way. We had dinner and breakfast and saw two movies while we traveled. Thirteen hours passed until we arrived in Taipei at

Charlotte writing in her journal. This chapter is made up of notes that she took during the trip.

7:05pm on Sunday, April 23 for a fuel stop. It was finally dark, but we couldn't get off the plane.

Monday, April 24, 1989

It's a sunny and warm day. We cashed in our traveler's checks numbers RZ129-925-137 and RZ129-925-138 to buy two suits, a coat, and a blazer from Princeton Custom Taylor. The prices are incredible.

We are a part of Lotus Tours. Phoenix, our tour host, gave us information and packets for our China Tour and we also left passports with her for our Visa to get into China. She will return them to us this evening at the hotel.

At 11:15AM we took pictures of Hong Kong from Tsim Sha Tsui, an urban area of Kowloon, Hong Kong. The pictures include those taken from the junk we were on. They are of downtown with buildings being renovated—they use bamboo poles for scaffolding. We took a ferry to Hong Kong Island and walked in the sun to the Hilton. We had lunch overlooking the harbor. What a beautiful view and an excellent lunch.

Tuesday, April 25, 1989

Our tour guide was Peggy. We went through the Cross-Harbour Tunnel which was the first tunnel in Hong Kong that was built underwater. It was built in 1972. It travels two kilometers through downtown Hong Kong to the downtown financial center. We took the tram to the top at 10:15AM. The view of the harbor was magnificent. We bought postcards and stamps. We traveled back down in a bus.

We walked through an outside bazaar for 45 min.

Roll #4 is on the bus to Aberdeen that used to be a thriving fishing village and still shows tranquil beauty. It's on the southern side of Hong Kong Island. It had the first harbor

Norm and Charlotte at the Jumbo Floating Restaurant

that European explorers came to. There are still people who live on boats in floating villages. They dry fish & squid in their villages.

After our trip around the harbor we went to a jewelry factory. Then a tunnel to Happy Valley, the most expensive area of Hong Kong.

We found out that certain numbers are believed to be connected to certain things. Number 4 means death in Chinese superstition. Number 8 is very lucky and means wealth, and the #10 is perfect. Red symbolizes good fortune and joy and Green is associated with health prosperity and harmony. We passed Happy Valley Race Track. Green Valley is surrounded by tall buildings.

Peggy recommends a restaurant that serves good fish, it's called Golden Birds Nest. It's in the Star House next to Star Ferry.

At 3:00pm we took a taxi to the site. Long trip – frequent traffic jams – to new territories – many high rises close together – clothes hanging on bamboo poles outside apt – no dryers. Electricity was too expensive to have dryers. We saw a pagoda building that was very brightly painted. The old Chinese roads are very narrow. There was a rapid transit train that traveled alongside the roads. We saw old autos that were in dumps alongside the road. There were farms of corn and rice. I saw old shacks and old buildings next to brand new construction that was not finished yet. It looks like the 21st century has invaded some other era.

Clothes hanging on bamboo poles outside apartments

Wednesday, April 26, 1989

We used travelers check #RZ129-925-135 for $100 to pay for suits & a coat along with a fitting because they make it all by hand and they want to make sure they fit. We walked all around Kowloon, through a hotel that had a unique ceiling. We found a Catholic Church on Chatham Road that was not far. There is a healing mass this evening at 8:00. It's an old building and needs refurbishing. There are many vases of fresh flowers and their statues are well-kept.

We had lunch at the Sheraton and then I wrote 12 post cards. I now need stamps.

Norm wrote in my journal:

TRAVERELS CHECKS TAKEN TO CHINA

RZ 129 925 149, 145, 146, 147, 148

In his wonderful block handwriting so we can keep track of the travelers checks we spend.

Thursday, April 27, 1989

We were taken to the airport by our travel guide. Once again there are people of all nationalities. Our plane is a 747, which is large, and it was probably full when it left because it seems packed. The stewardesses are very businesslike.

It was a very choppy flight with clouds all around the plane almost all the way into Beijing. When clouds cleared enough for us to see, we were over very flat land that looked like the United States Midwest. As the plane came down, we could see groupings of buildings that looked like a neutral color, which was probably brick. The land had some green, what I assumed was grass or rice fields and had gray long aluminum topped buildings.

Beijing Airport was crowded so we stood in line for a long time waiting to go through customs. The room was long and dark with construction on the side of the building. There were so many smokers polluting the air. The bags that were coming onto the luggage belt were unloaded from the airlines and they contained TV's, VCRs, and other electronics from Hong Kong. We waited a long time for our bags and as we waited we met a couple from the Philippines; Fernando and Winnie. They will be with Memory Tours – guide found all 4 of us and took us in a twelve-passenger van with a driver. She explained what we were seeing. The road was excellent. On our way we saw many trees and shrubs that were planted along the highway. There was green grass in the medians and winter wheat fields extending for miles. We had to pull over as a police car was guiding about 6 Mercedes down the highway. Fernando said the Asian Bank Development Commission was meeting in Beijing so there were probably VIPs in town. The guide said that because of the students massing in Tiananmen Square, we'll probably go to the Great Wall on Friday instead of Saturday.

Our motel is called Beijing-Toronto and is a joint venture with Toronto, Canada. The room reminds me of Holiday Inns during our trip to Louisiana with the boat. The carpet is dirty, but the bed and bathrooms are clean. The beds are hard but comfortable. We're staying on the 11th floor and can watch people from our windows as they catch buses, walk on both sides of the boulevard – are they commuting? Are they just strolling?

We were very tired, so we went to bed at 9:00pm.

Friday, April 28, 1989

After breakfast we left at 9am to go to the tomb of Emperor called Dingling Tomb. We met a Philippine couple from California named Tom and Carol. We also met Barbara and Susy from New York. Including us, there are eight on the tour. And as we know, the number 8 is very lucky number. The excavation reveals a 400-year-old burial tombs of an Emperor, his first wife, and his concubines. We couldn't take pictures inside.

After lunch we took a bus through the mountains seeing green fields, brick buildings, and very dry grasses. It's been a dry season. And then we arrived at The Great Wall of China where we took lots of pictures.

> The Ming Tombs:
> The Ming Tombs lie on the south slope of the Tianshou Mountain. This is the imperial burial place of thirteen emperors of the Ming dynasty. The mausoleums opened to tourists are Changling and Dingling. Dingling, the tomb of Emperor Zhu Yijun, is the only one of the Ming Tombs excavated so far. The relics displayed in the exhibition rooms include gold crown, phoenix crown and dragon robe. *

Norm walked up all the way on the left side of the stairs where it's supposed to be a steeper climb than the right side. I climbed along about ¾ way up then sat and watched people and waited for Norm. He reported a ski lift was being built that he could see from the top.

What a view and an accomplishment! On our way back, we saw some of the wall that had not been refurbished. The difference was striking.

There were tour buses all over the place. Since people all over the world come to see that view, including residents of China, the amount of people crowded into the area was remarkable.

The Great Wall of China

As we drove back, we noticed that coal trucks coming from Outer Mongolia used the same highway as the Great Wall exit.

Our trip back was long. Our driver was stopped by the police and fined for a traffic infraction. He was supposed to stay in truck/bus lane and not pass traffic at a certain point, but he did. And he was caught.

Charlotte on the right, walking up the stairs at The Great Wall of China.

That night we had supper in a restaurant with other tourists from Binghamton, NY. We celebrated one of their birthdays, ate way too much food that was served family style, and tried to identify some of the food we were eating as it was non-descript.

After dinner we went to the theater. A group of young people danced authentic cultural dances, played musical instruments from past dynasties, and sang songs that were translated on a screen that was on the wall. They had beautiful colorful costumes that enthralled us so much that we took lots and lots of pictures.

Saturday, April 29, 1989

9:00am: It is smoggy, and the streets are filled with bicyclists and walkers. Main Street

Cultural dance in the theater

is 40 kilometers (24 miles) long. Today is our day to go to Tiananmen Square. There are tourists all around, and it looks like the students are resting today. About Tiananmen Square our guidebooks says:

> Tiananmen Square
> The magnificent Tiananmen is the symbol of new Beijing and new China. The square is 880 meters long from north to south and 500 meters wide from east to west. In the center of the square stands the Monument to the People's Heroes, which is 37.94 meters high and is composed of 413 pieces of granite. It is the hugest monument in the Chinese history. On the south side is the solemn Chairman Mao's Memorial Hall. The Museum of Chinese History and the Museum of the Chinese Revolution are on the eastern side of Tiananmen Square. *

Our guide told us that on October 1, 1949 Mao Zedong named himself head of state and officially proclaimed the existence of the People's Republic of China. This proclamation was the peak of many years of battle between Mao's communist forces and Chinese Nationalism led by Chiang Kai-Shek, who had been supported with money and arms from the American government. The proclamation happened right here in Tiananmen Square.

Tiananmen Square on Saturday, April 29, 1989

Sun Yat-sen is another important Chinese leader. He was born November 2, 1866 and died March 12, 1925. He was a leader of the Chinese Nationalist Party and is known as the father of modern China. He was influential in the overthrowing of the Qing (Manchu) dynasty in 1911/12 and served as the first provisional president of the Republic of China (1911/12) and then as its de facto ruler (1923-25). For those who believe in this government he is celebrated. For those who don't, they protest in their own way, much like the students are doing in Tiananmen Square. Peaceful and within their own respectful way. Students gathering to send a message. But not today. They are all resting today.

The day is warm as we start on the Forbidden City Tour, which is an area of Beijing where two dynasties lived. It's a 15th century palace complex that was once the royal residence. They were so suspicious of traitors that they took all the trees down so nobody could hide from view. Inside there were marble slabs, glazed ceramic tile, huge urns, and incense burners burning incense. The smell was overwhelming. Some

Charlotte and Norm at Tiananmen Square

of the rooms inside were blocked off and there were people everywhere. We saw a Tibetan couple that were with each tour that comes through the area.

After lunch, we went through the Summer Palace. It had been refurbished recently and the colors were brighter than the

Summer Palace

buildings that weren't newly refurbished. There were lots of boats on the lake.

A marble boat is set in place because the empress got seasick.

The Summer Palace is one of the existing imperial gardens on a large scale. In 1860 it was destroyed by British and French Allied Forces. Then, in 1888, Empress Dowager Cixi embezzled more than 5 million Liang silver from Navy funds to rebuild it. Inside the garden there is Wenzhou Shan, the Longevity Hill, the Long Corridor, The Hall of Buddhist incense, the Bronze Pavilion, the Marble Boat as well as the Garden of Harmonious Interests, the Seventeen Arches Bridge, the gilt Bronze Ox and the Spring Showing Pavilion.

As we ride in the van, we see so much construction. There are tall cranes on tall buildings that look like they're planting big trees and little trees all over. They are building several parks along the way and we noticed huts, brick one-story houses, and lots of land planted with crops. They are laying huge drains along some very good highways.

Sunday, April 30, 1989

The day is cool. Leang and our driver met us at the hotel at 6:15am: Carol and Ed, Winnie and Ferdinand, and us. They drove us to a military airport where we caught a plane for Xi'an. The plane left at 7:35am.

Once we arrived in Xi'an (Sian, Shian) Hi met us and we stopped for coffee. We found out that it had rained for 3 days and that was why it was a cool day. With all the rain comes green foliage. With that cool weather, we were comfortable.

There was lots of construction all around. We then drove through the countryside. There were green winter wheat fields, rivers, a primitive road in areas. On our way, we saw lots of bicycles and trucks and buses. Once we arrived, we saw people gathering at intersections, looking like they were socializing for their Sunday and had come to see the Terra Cotta Army, just like us. We took many pictures outside but couldn't take any in the museum. Our pictures are taken inside the dig area and are completely unbelievable!!!!!

After seeing the Terra Cotta Army, we were treated to a very impressive lunch of Chinese Foods. We then went to Banpo Dig where the archeologists have reconstructed area of 6000-year-old commune village. There are skeletons, pottery and other utensils. Many explanations of life at that time. Also showed very beginning of Chinese written language.

For dinner we had Chinese food, it wasn't as good as lunch, but it was ok because I was hungry.

My left shoulder hurt from hunching in van, I guess. So, we relaxed in the hotel lobby of Hotel Jinhua and had a drink while we listened to a string quartet.

While sleeping that night I dreamt I was going to get acupuncture. It must have been because my left shoulder hurt so badly.

Monday, May 1, 1989

We had breakfast at the hotel and left at 9:30am to see the commune. It was May Day and we saw lots of bicyclists and people walking, enjoying their day. Maybe family outing day because it was May Day. The weather was comfortable – clear, maybe 70 degrees.

They told us this was a Commune – saw someone's home and I figure that name doesn't really make sense; really, it's a township because it contains factories, schools, acupuncture, massage, and a hospital. We went inside so Ed could see everything and how primitive it all is. There were fields of wheat and soybeans. There were small children that were very friendly. There were donkeys hauling wagons and dragging wagons. They carried heavy loads like dirt, rocks, tiles, and the like.

They demonstrated machine embroidery and then we went through the selling area which was a courtyard in the center.

Lunch was western style. There was rice, steak, cauliflower, and coffee. And for dessert there was cake.

Then off to the Giant Wild Goose Pagoda. It's a Buddhist pagoda from 600AD during the Tang Dynasty. We climbed up to the top and took pictures from landing. There were a lot of people in the area of the Buddist Pagoda. Lots of people were staring at us. I wondered what they were thinking about the Americans looking at their pagoda.

From there we went to old wall from 1500s. climbed stairs. Took pictures – park surrounding wall with people all over – came back to hotel to rest and read Noble House by James Clavell.

We then met in the lobby and walked along road in front

Charlotte and Norm having a wonderful time

of hotel, enjoying our last night in Xi'an. We had an evening drink with everyone as we planned the next morning. We needed to have our bags ready by 5:30 am and outside our door to be placed on the van to go to the airport. Breakfast is at 6:00am in the hotel and we will leave at 6:30am for the airport. The plane to Guangzhou (also known as Canton, the capital and most populous city of the province of Guangdong) leaves at 8:45 am. With that plan in mind, we went to bed and slept soundly.

Tuesday, May 2, 1989

We were up at 4:30am, our luggage was picked up at 5:30, just as planned. Breakfast at 6:00 am. To the airport for our 6:30am flight from Xi'an to Canton. It was good flight. The sky was partly cloudy. The land below the plane was both mountainous and then flat. The closer we got to Canton, the more water we saw. Land below mountains and flat – closer to Canton. Lots of water.

Canton is located in southern China and is on the Pearl River. When we landed, our Lotus Tours guide told us that a large thunder storm with lots of rain had just passed through. And now that it was sunny and humid, it felt very much like Louisiana. We took a taxi to Sun Yat Sen Memorial Hall. It is a large octagonal structure with a span of 71 meters without pillars, housing a large stage and seats many people. The old Chinese architecture creates perfect sound for the stage. We then had lunch at a restaurant that had very good Cantonese Food.

Then on to Chen Clan Classical Academy where we saw magnificent carvings and museum pieces built 2000 years ago by the Chen Clan to house them during their preparations for the imperial examination during the Qing Dynasty. They still use it when necessary, but it has been changed to the Chen Clan's Industry College. We saw all kinds of intricate carvings, hand embroidery, and beautiful painting from provinces around China.

As this hot and humid day came to an end, we were happy to settle in our hotel called The White Swan. It was large and so very comfortable. We had dinner in the oldest restaurant in town: Happy Happy.

Wednesday, May 3, 1989

It was a smoggy day in Canton. While we ate breakfast, we watched the boats and sampans as well as other river transportation on The Pearl River. We then checked out of The White Swan. Our Lotus Tours guide took us to the train station where we caught a train to Hong Kong. We sat in car number 11. It began to rain along the way and Norm took lots of pictures of the lush farmlands, banana trees, rice fields, and other crops. Once we got there, we went through customs in the train station and was then picked up by a man from Lotus Tours. He brought us to the Sheraton Hotel. It was 3:30pm and our room wasn't ready.

As it rained, we went to Princeton Custom Taylor to pick up the suits, jackets and coat that we had ordered when we arrived. We paid for them. The ocean terminal was recommended to us for a good place to buy toys. When we saw that there was a Toys R Us, same as in the US, we smiled.

Thursday, May 4, 1989

Saw Japan Cruise ship at terminal – went to watch the ships leave from their industrial center.

We took a bouquet of flowers to Phoenix at Lotus Tours to thank her for all her hard work. She wasn't there so we left the flowers and a message.

Ben called to confirm our flight times. We'll leave the hotel at noon for the airport and they'll pick us up.

We rested for a while before we walked to mass at Rosary Church. On the way to mass, we saw blocks of students with banners shouting. We couldn't tell what they were saying but it must have been in support of democracy and the end to corruption in Beijing.

We went to 6:15pm mass that was said in Chinese. We said one decade of the Rosary after mass. At 10:00pm, Phoenix called to tell us that she would meet us in the lobby in the morning and have breakfast with us.

Friday, May 5, 1989

Phoenix brought me a gift of two combs and two ink sticks with a Phoenix bird on the side of it. Jacky from Lotus Tours took us to the airport in a Mercedes limousine and helped us get started. We went into the United Airlines hospitality room to wait for our plane flight.

We left Hong Kong at 2:00pm and it was cloudy all the way across the Pacific and into Seattle.

Tiananmen Square Massacre

Only a month after we had seen Tiananmen Square, the protests that we witnessed culminated on the night of June 3-4 with a government crackdown. Although there were government repression protests throughout China, the students in Tiananmen Square became the symbol of what the next generation can do for their country. By 1989, many Chinese youth had been exposed to foreign ideas and standards of living and they knew what life could be like. Their government was failing them even through the economic advances that China was experiencing. But those advances led to prices being inflated and corrupt government officials. Because of universal advancements, the students felt like they had a voice. And they spoke up only to be silenced by their government, the Chinese Communist Party. Our generation had questioned whether the Communists would put an end to the demonstrations. We are so used to them shutting their people down. We were proud of the students, but worried about them as demonstrations continued throughout May. And then on June 3rd, troops and security police began to indiscriminately fire on the students. As the students tried to escape, the forces continued their rampage. Some of the protesters fought back by throwing rocks and overturning and setting fire to military vehicles. By the next day when the square was cleared, at least 300 protesters were killed and over 10,000 were arrested. This ended the Tiananmen protests with a massacre of not only the students and residents of Beijing, but also of their dreams for a democratic future for China. *

Marathon Walk

I never did count how many miles I drove in my yellow Ford Ranchero while I drove back and forth between Albany, Salem, and Portland. Now after five years working at Albany Farm Supply the job was finally finished. How do I change my routine?

I started each morning by walking through our neighborhood in southeast Portland.

As the days went by, my walks took me longer distances from home and I enjoyed seeing men proudly checking their flower beds and women sweeping their porches with vigor. They all returned my smile and a good morning in whatever language they spoke.

There was always a little café that was new to me and a place to rest my tired feet and have a good cup of coffee and lunch along the way. The walk back home became interesting as I would find many new things to see in new neighborhoods.

When I arrived home, I would take all my sore muscles to the bathroom and run warm water into my bathtub, add peppermint salts and get in for a long soak.

This new routine went on from Monday to Friday for months, rain or shine. It was very important for me to change my schedule from driving to work every day to being home.

The following January I found an ad in the local newspaper that looked like it would be an interesting adventure.

WOMEN LEARNING TO WALK THE MARATHON NINE MONTHS OF CLASSES CALL THIS PHONE NUMBER

The Portland Marathon would be run at the end of September.

As I had been walking a leisurely gait for months, I thought this sounded like something I could do.

I went to the introductory session. Most of the women seemed to be in their late 30's, 40's or 50's. As I was 67 I asked Penny if this was possible for me to accomplish.

She told me that one of the ladies was in her early 70's.

As the instructions were given and questions answered I was impressed with the visible enthusiasm. Penny told us all about the routine for walking each Saturday and the next Saturday we would walk a mile.

During each session we were given the plans for that day.

The mile went very well. It was a good time to become better acquainted with this new routine and the other walkers.

The next Saturday assignment would be a five-mile walk with a chance to turn back at the three-mile marker. As we walked on a flat surface near the Willamette River and into the industrial area, the walk became tiring and a small group of us decided to turn back.

So now I had a new routine. Each Saturday morning at 4 AM I had an oatmeal and fruit breakfast, put a bagel and a slice of cheese in a zip lock bag, got a bottle of water and my jacket and hat for the day's walk and drove to the walk site for the day.

As the weeks went by, we would either walk through the hills to Forest Park or up curvy Terwilliger highway to the hospital or in Gresham along the Springwater corridor or on the bridge over I-5 Highway to Lewis and Clark University and into the trails through the park and back.

The weather was mild during some of the Saturday mornings that winter. Other mornings were foggy and some days the rain came down in buckets. By afternoon usually the rain would let up and even sometimes the sun would shine brightly in the clear air. The walks were always challenging.

The leader for that day, and her fit friends, were always showing us where to go. As we walked we talked to whoever was walking the same pace that we were. Laughter could be heard along the way as jokes were traded or a TV comedy recalled or a funny situation from people's homes.

With so many runners and walkers using the Springwater trail sometimes the bathroom facilities along the way were clean and sometimes they were in dire need of large maintenance crews. Some Saturdays we were the only group walking the trail. Other times families or groups of classmates training for track meets or cross-country competitions would share the pathway.

One of these walks went along for a mile or so when my knee started to get very painful. I sat down at the next bench we came to and a kind lady of our group said she had a remedy for my pain. She brought out a bottle of Tylenol from her pocket. I took one and continued walking. After a while I was pleasantly surprised as the pain lessened.

That's just the way it was. Someone in the group always had a suggestion that helped whatever the problem.

One of the mornings on the Springwater corridor path we passed an old ramshackle building which had been a brickyard. I had never seen a place where bricks were made, and one excited new friend proceeded to tell us all about the production of bricks. At the back of the shed were layers and layers of red dusty bricks.

Those months of getting our bodies and minds ready went fast and finally the time came to plan our attack of walking the marathon. We were excited as Penny gave us the schedule for the morning of The Portland Marathon.

I followed my same routine of breakfast, snack and water, hat and jacket and was off to downtown Portland. When I arrived, there were many walkers and runners stretching out. We had learned early on how important stretching was to get the muscles ready for the long or short distance.

The waves of walkers started out first so as to be out of the way of the runners in the crowded downtown streets.

As we walked the marked path, there were many encouraging voices coming from the water stations and other people with timers.

The beginning of the run took us to a route that we had already walked during our training, over the railroad tracks, through an industrial section, then along the river.

Heading west, the sudden view of the St. John's Bridge arching high over the Willamette River was impressive and the sun began to shine bringing warmth to the early morning.

As we turned off St. Helen's Road onto the bridge, we walked to the middle of the span and stopped to enjoy the calm river and the Cathedral Park far below us. Others passed me as we all started our fast pace again. One friend stayed with me as she said I should not walk alone. I assured her that I would be alright and for her to go on and do her best.

Since they were ahead of me, I could see where they had turned at the end of the bridge and I followed. The road went up small hills into some of the first neighborhoods where the early settlers had come to work in N. Portland. By this time, I was walking alone and admiring the fall flowers growing in the gardens of the neighborhoods.

Both of my knees had become more painful and I found I could not out-walk the pain.

Now I started asking myself, "How much longer are you going to try to go on. Are you trying to prove something? Is your health in jeopardy?"

As I was talking to myself I came to one of the signposts of the marathon: a bench on a hill in front of the University of Portland. I sat a while and nothing felt better so I decided I didn't have anything to prove to myself. I had had a very productive time learning to walk the marathon, had met great women during my endeavor, and I should be satisfied with what I had accomplished in walking almost 20 miles.

My husband told me to call him if I needed something, so I did and he came to pick me up. I waited for him on that bench in the serene park-like scenery of the University of Portland, a Catholic University along the north side of the Willamette River.

Family Heritage

Our family heritage and the formation of the German Schwab family was based on the Benedictine values and the Rule of Benedict which were written by the Saint Benedict of Nursia around the year 529 AD. When I was born in 1929, the Benedictine way of life had been part of our family life for over 100 years. When the Schwab family settled in the Mt Angel area in the mid 1800's, the Benedictine way of life was the basic structure of how our family worshiped, raised our families, and lived our everyday lives. After initial settlement with other German immigrants, we requested that the Benedictine priests and sisters come from the motherland to create parishes, catholic schools, and monasteries. And, most importantly, help us form strong communities with Benedictine teaching, values, and structure. Although I don't remember any formal training in the rule of Benedict, this way of life was just who we were and how we lived. We were very

"Benedictine" by design. Norm and I chose very carefully and discussed often how we wanted to raise our children and felt by giving them the gift of faith, and a strong belief in God and his almighty power, that they would have a strong life structure. They would have a belief system that was solid, and a heritage that would help them raise their families and give them the strength to prevail in any dark moments or low points in life.

Marriage

Often times when people saw Norm and I walk together, holding hands, they would ask us, "What is the key to a good marriage?" They would hear that we had 10 children, or they would see the family together (well-behaved children all of them), and their curiosity about us would lead them to ask these types of questions. How do we do it? And how do we maintain it?

The answer would be immediate: we are best friends. We deeply love each other. We share a common religion and viewpoint of life. We agree with how we should live and how to enjoy life. We didn't try to influence or control each other. We respected each other's individual freedoms, viewpoints, and feelings. And we were eager to share life's experiences with one another.

We didn't nag or take out a bad day on each other. We didn't try to impress or keep up with others. There was no political arguing, actually no arguing at all. We talked a lot but never argued. Because, what is the point of arguing with your best friend?

We looked at the relationship through a positive lens. We thought a positive outlook and attitude would produce the best results for us and our family. These traits were, to some degree, formed through experiences that we had while growing up in our own families. Norm never liked it when his brothers and sisters argued. He would say to me, "People seemed to justify arguing by being the devil's advocate. That never produces or proves anything."

I was never big on gossip because I feel it only tears people down and, again, never produces anything. I guess you would say that we felt we could use our time in a better way.

We also took marriage very seriously, we deeply felt it was a sacrament not just a paper license issued by a local government official. As Catholics, we felt that the sacraments were very carefully produced by the Church. We believe that they are the words of Jesus, spoken through the apostles and communicated to us through their written word. If God thought they were so important that his only son spoke of them, then that was good enough for us.

Our faith was our strength and the core strength in our marriage.

As we woke up each morning we would ask ourselves, "What can I do to make the day better for you?" Sometimes it was just letting me sleep because he could see that I was exhausted. Sometimes it was a hug in the kitchen or holding my hand when I needed it. We always had each other's welfare at heart.

We feel that kindness to each other, and others, produces the best results and is the right thing to do.

I sure miss him!

Dedication to Family

Very early, after I met Norm, we discussed how important family is to us. My father, Paul Schwab, came from a big family all living within blocks of each other in Mt. Angel, Oregon. My grandfather's company, The Fred Schwab Commission Company, employed and supported the whole Schwab clan within that farming community of Mt Angel. After my father died, I rarely observed as much happiness as when he was alive.

When I met Norm's family, I was very pleased to see a happy family. As Norm and I spoke more about having a large family, we decided that a happy family with love at the center would be our choice.

The Schwab and Schmidt families, along with the family reunions, were a big part of our social life. I am joyful when I see the legacy continuing with my children, grandchildren and now great grandchildren! I feel our family is unique because love is at the center. Even as you are all different, you always set aside those differences, never judge and you choose to love.

God has blessed our family with good health, wisdom, common sense and most importantly the gift of faith. For without God, life and family can have little substance or meaning.

I am proud our family is the symbol of love and giving, we encourage and support each other and touch each other's hearts with God's love.

Schwab Family Reunion in Mt. Angel, OR. August 2017
Back row: Amy, Ric, Frank, Ellen, Carolyn, Sarah, Martha
Front row: Jake, Charlotte, Donna, LuAnn

A letter to you from Charlotte

Norm is in heaven and I miss him so. We lived many years together and I will always be thankful that God put him in my life. And, oh!, what a wonderful blessed life it has been! I'm enjoying retirement in Palm Desert, California. The warmth, dryness and spiritual openness of the desert extends my life and I hope to live many more productive years.

I'd like my family to know that I think about them all the time as I sit in my desert home. It brings me great joy to send birthday and Christmas cards to everyone through the years. To my 29 grand and great grandchildren, as well as my children and their spouses and my many relatives and friends, I love you all.

I'd also like to thank everyone who helped put this book together. I'd especially like to thank Tammy Coia, my memoir writing teacher, and the other ladies in our class. You all helped bring out these remarkable stories. Thank you so much!

My prayers are always with all my loved ones. I pray that we focus on taking care of one another, encouraging each other, and spreading love and joy with a smile! May God Bless all of you!

September 1, 2018

The Fisher Family

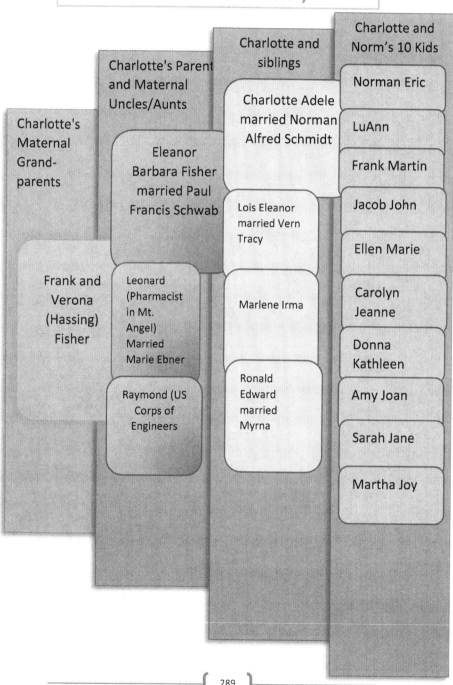

Charlotte's Maternal Grandparents

Frank and Verona (Hassing) Fisher

Charlotte's Parents and Maternal Uncles/Aunts

Eleanor Barbara Fisher married Paul Francis Schwab

Leonard (Pharmacist in Mt. Angel) Married Marie Ebner

Raymond (US Corps of Engineers

Charlotte and siblings

Charlotte Adele married Norman Alfred Schmidt

Lois Eleanor married Vern Tracy

Marlene Irma

Ronald Edward married Myrna

Charlotte and Norm's 10 Kids

Norman Eric

LuAnn

Frank Martin

Jacob John

Ellen Marie

Carolyn Jeanne

Donna Kathleen

Amy Joan

Sarah Jane

Martha Joy

The Schwab Family

Charlotte's Paternal Grandparents

Frederick Schwab and Anna Mary Mayer

Charlotte's Parents and Paternal Uncles/Aunts

Mary Josephine Schwab married Louis Anthony LeDoux

Gertrude Beatrice Schwab married Harry Ben Craig (Maxine's parents)

Joseph Benedict (Uncle Joe) Schwab married Mary Louise Kerr

Agnes Caroline Schwab married Clyde Eugene Lindsey

Paul Francis Schwab married Eleanor Barbara Fisher

Rose Anne Schwab married Joseph Wachter

Leo A. Schwab married Lauretta Louise Clouse (cousin Larry's parents)

Louis A. Schwab married Delores Kruse

Amanda Marie Schwab married Albert Theodore Wilde

Charlotte and siblings

Charlotte Adele married Norman Alfred Schmidt

Lois Eleanor married Vernon Tracy

Marlene Irma married John Roger Hoy

Ronald Edward married Myrna Seavy

Charlotte and Norm's 10 Kids

Norman Eric

LuAnn

Frank Martin

Jacob John

Ellen Marie

Carolyn Jeanne

Donna Kathleen

Amy Joan

Sarah Jane

Martha Joy

Index

My index is organized by page number. Unless otherwise specified in the index, the pictures printed in this book either came from Charlotte's photo albums or were saved by her mother, Eleanor. Eleanor kept every picture she had. She also kept newspaper articles, condolence cards, and funeral cards. The newspaper articles were copies from the originals that were in her things. If the information within this book was gathered somewhere besides Charlotte or Eleanor's possessions, they are cited here:

picture I found here:
www.travelsalem.com/node/42160

48: Information about the earthquake came from The Statesman Journal, an article written by Andy Zimmerman on March 25, 2015. You can find the full article on: www.statesmanjournal.com/story/life/2015/03/22/spring-break-quake-led-lasting-changes/25065255/

63: Picture of The Creamery was found in the best place for me to get historical pictures about Mt. Angel: http://www.mtangelhistory.org/

66: Depression information from: www.history.com/topics/great-depression

69: Rheumatic Fever information from the Mayo Clinic at: www.mayoclinic.org/diseases-conditions/rheumatic-fever/symptoms-causes/syc-20354588

92: Information about Last Rites was written by Amy Webber and is general knowledge.

97: Information about Western Oregon University is found on their web page: www.wou.edu

103: Information about John Philip Sousa is found online. Just ask the Marines! www.marineband.marines.mil/About/Our-History/John-Philip-Sousa/

195: This trailer picture was found online, I just Googled trailers of that era and found it on this webpage: https://tincantourists.com/wiki/doku.php?id=yellowstone
But, since they made their trip before I was even born, I don't know what it actually looked like. Of course, you can ask one of my older siblings, but they will probably say that this one is pretty close to the original. Of course, it doesn't show eight people piled inside of it, so maybe it's not as accurate as I wanted it to be.

198 Paul Bunyan picture found on The Trees of Mystery website. www.treesofmystery.net/paul-babe.php

218 Columbus Day Storm information found: https://en.wikipedia.org/wiki/Columbus_Day_Storm_of_1962

223: For the map of the US, I grabbed a map from www.ontheworldmap.com and created the trip from Portland to Kentucky.

228: The recipe for Kentucky Bourbon Balls is mine. I'm sure I got it somewhere, I just don't remember where. (At the time of this writing, I had some bourbon balls in my refrigerator from Christmas.) When Mom and her friends made them when we were little, I would eat as much as I could since I loved them so much. The story is that I would ask Mom for one and she would say, "Yes, but just one." So, I would eat one. Then I would go from sibling to sibling asking if they would like any. If they said that they would, I'd go back to the candy bin, get one for them, and take one for me. Now, I doubt if that actually happened, because I was a good little girl, but since I remember those bourbon balls with such happiness, I have a feeling that story may be at least partially true.

239: Picture of the Albany Farm Supply building is on the Albany Regional Museum website. www.armuseum.com

243: I got the picture of the King Sisters online at: www.hollywoodreporter.com/news/ marilyn-king-last-of-singing-sisters-602702

It's from an article written by Mike Barnes on 8/8/2013 for The Hollywood Reporter

271 and 273:   The information about the Ming Tombs and Tiananmen Square is taken directly from the map that Mom and Dad brought from their trip. It was given them by their tour guide.

281:   Online information about Tiananmen Square: www.britannica.com/event/Tiananmen-Square-incident

Thanks for reading Mom's book! It was a pleasure to edit it.

I would like to thank the above websites for letting me use their information and pictures. Thank you.

And thank you to Charlotte Adele Schwab Schmidt for sharing her amazing life with us! We love you! God bless you always and always!

Amy Joan Schmidt Webber

89381751R00190

Made in the USA
San Bernardino, CA
24 September 2018